15

Books
date ca
week
Books
anothe

ALL L
Bank Ho

15

a Sunday Times series

Handbook for the
VAUXHALL VICTOR 101
AND VX4/90
FC SERIES
from 1964

PIET OLYSLAGER MSIA MSAE

NELSON

THOMAS NELSON AND SONS LTD

36 Park Street London W1
P.O. Box 336 Apapa Lagos
P.O. Box 25012 Nairobi
P.O. Box 21149 Dar es Salaam
77 Coffee Street San Fernando Trinidad

THOMAS NELSON (AUSTRALIA) LTD
597 Little Collins Street Melbourne

THOMAS NELSON AND SONS (CANADA) LTD
81 Curlew Drive Don Mills Ontario

THOMAS NELSON AND SONS (SOUTH AFRICA) (PTY) LTD
P.O. Box 9881 Johannesburg

THOMAS NELSON AND SONS
Copewood and Davis Streets Camden 3, N.J

English language edition

© OLYSLAGER ORGANISATION N.V. 1967

Printed in Gt. Britain by GALLEON PRINTERS LIMITED, HAZEL GROVE, CHESHIRE

iv

Contents

SPECIAL NOTE

Although every care is taken to ensure accuracy and completeness in compiling this book, no liability can be accepted for damage, loss or injury caused by any errors or omissions in the information given.

Preface

THIS MANUAL is intended to supplement (not to replace) the instruction book issued with the car by the manufacturer. It contains more detailed information on the maintenance and repair of the Victor 101 and VX 4/90 without being, or pretending to be, a fully comprehensive workshop manual.

The early sections of the book contain general information essential for both owner-driver and mechanic. They give full details about the models covered so that the reader does not have to refer to many different publications in order to find correct model designations, serial numbers, major modifications, prices, dimensions, lubrication, maintenance and other information.

The section *Repair Data* has been compiled and presented on the assumption that the reader knows something about repair work. Elementary procedures have therefore been omitted and the space has been devoted to more advanced information. Readers who are not qualified to carry out repairs and adjustments are strongly advised to leave them to official Vauxhall dealers or distributors, whose mechanics possess special equipment and are fully informed about the latest modifications and design changes. Often it will be more economical to replace a component by either a new or a factory-reconditioned unit rather than attempt to repair it. In all cases of doubt it will pay to consult a dealer.

All the important dimensions, tolerances and other specifications are presented in convenient tabular form at the end of the book, followed by an engine fault-finding chart.

PIET OLYSLAGER, MSAE, MSAI

Fig. 1. Victor 101 model FCS (basic) Saloon, 1964-66

Fig. 2. Victor 101 model FCD Super Saloon, 1966-67

VAUXHALL VICTOR 101 and VX 4/90

FC Series from 1964

General

INTRODUCTION

The Victor 101 and VX 4/90 FC Series were introduced by Vauxhall Motors Ltd., Luton, England, in October, 1964, to replace the FB Series which had been in production since 1961. Compared with the FB, the FC models offer more room, more comfort and greater refinement, brought about by a major re-design.

As in the Victor FB Series, there are two basic body types, namely four-door Saloons and Estate Cars, in six different styles, as listed below.

1966 and 1967 models, officially introduced in October 1965 and October 1966 respectively, differ only in detail from the original models (see under Modifications).

'Super Traction' limited slip differential and 'Powerglide' automatic transmission became available as optional extras in May and June, 1965, respectively. From September 1965 'Super Traction' is standard equipment on the VX 4/90 Saloon.

Summary of models:

FCS — Victor 101 (basic) four-door, four/five-passenger Saloon
FCD — Victor 101 Super four-door, four/five-passenger Saloon
FCE — Victor 101 De Luxe four-door, four/five-passenger Saloon
FCW — Victor 101 Super four-door, four/five-passenger Estate Car
FCG — Victor 101 De Luxe four-door, four/five-passenger Estate Car
FCH — VX 4/90 four-door, four/five-passenger Saloon

DESCRIPTION

The Victor 101 FC model, the body of which is a completely new design, is powered by a four-cylinder overhead-valve engine of 1595cc cubic capacity. Except for a higher compression ratio (9·0 instead of 8·5 to 1), this engine is basically the same as that which was introduced in September 1963 for the 1964 FB models. The VX 4/90 has a twin-carburettor version of the same engine, with a compression ratio of 9·3 to 1. Carburettors are of Zenith manufacture.

Victor 101 models have a three- or (optional) four-speed all-synchromesh gearbox, and the latter is standard on the VX 4/90. The VX 4/90 has disc front brakes with vacuum servo assistance, which is optional equipment on Victor models.

All models have a unitary body-cum-chassis with curved side windows. The body finish, applied over primer coats, is 'Magic Mirror' acrylic lacquer, which does not need polishing. The saloons have a double-curvature rear window. The main differences between the various models are listed below. See also under Modifications (page 8).

Body styles:

Basic Saloon (Victor 101 FCS, see Fig. 1): Standard saloon with bench-type front seat. Vynide seat upholstery. Full-width parcel shelf with central glove compartment under facia panel. Floor covering consisting of fitted rubber mats. Plain rubber window surrounds. Individual front seats (1964-66) and four-speed floor-change optional extras. Single horn and sun visor. Six single-tone body colours.

Super Saloon (Victor 101 FCD, see Fig. 2): As basic saloon but with bright mouldings in anodised aluminium, running the full length of the body sides, carpet floor

Fig. 3. Victor 101 model FCE De Luxe Saloon, 1964-66

Fig. 4. VX 4/90 model FCH Saloon, 1966-67

Fig. 5. VX 4/90 model FCH Saloon, threequarter rear view, 1964-66

covering, two sun visors, padding on the upper half of the facia panel, courtesy switches for the roof light, operated by the front doors, and 'Super' nameplate on luggage compartment lid. Nine single-tone body colours.

De Luxe Saloon (Victor 101 FCE, see Figs. 3 and 10): Individual, separately adjustable front seats, thickly padded and upholstered in soft 'Ambla' or leather (optional extra). Each door fitted with padded armrests; the rear door armrests incorporating ashtrays. Cut-pile carpeting with five layers of sound-deadening material on the floor. Heater/defroster and windscreen-washer as standard equipment. Dual horns and sun visors. Sliding door with lock for the glove compartment. Anodised aluminium roof-drip mouldings, wheel embellishers and special hub caps incorporating medallions. 1967 models have a bright sill moulding below the doors. 'De Luxe' nameplate on luggage compartment lid. Four-speed floor-change optional extra. Seven single and five two-tone body colours.

Super Estate Car (Victor 101 FCW, see Figs. 6, 7 and 8): Big one-piece tail door, hinged at the top and extending the full width of the car, with counterbalancing torsion bars for easy lifting. The cargo space measures 51·7 cubic feet and the floor area, with the rear seat folded down, is 53·7 inches wide by 69 inches long. Trim and equipment as on Super saloon. Five single and four two-tone body colours.

De Luxe Estate Car (Victor 101 FCG): As Super Estate Car but trim and equipment as De Luxe saloon. Carpeted cargo compartment and zip cover for the spare wheel. Choice of six single and four two-tone body colours.

Fig. 6. Victor 101 model FCW Super Estate Car, 1964-66

VX 4/90 Saloon (FCH, see Figs. 4, 5, 11 and front cover): High-performance saloon with 85·5 bhp twin-carburettor engine, four-speed gearbox, 'Super Traction' differential and front disc brakes. More luxuriously equipped than Victor 101 saloons. Individual front seats and floor gear change. Facia with four hooded dials, including rev counter. 'VX 4/90' designation on rear quarter panels (rear wings on 1967 models).

IDENTIFICATION

Engine number: The engine number is stamped on the right-hand side of the cylinder block, adjacent to the fuel pump. It is prefixed 30FC on Victor 101 FC30 engines, 31FC on VX 4/90 FC31 twin-carburettor engines.

Chassis number: The chassis serial number is stamped on a plate which is located on the inside of the left-hand wing valance in the engine compartment. This plate also gives, in code, the model designation, specification of trim, body colour, etc.

In August 1965, when production of the 1966 models commenced, a new numbering system was introduced. The chassis number consists of seven figures of which the last five are the actual serial number. The first two figures indicate the model year (6=1966, 7=1967 model) and the assembly plant (1=Luton, 5=Ellesmere Port, etc.). Example: 6112919, which is a Victor, 1966 model, produced in Luton in September 1965.

Chassis serial numbers (approximate, and for guidance only):

October 1964 (starting):	5001001
January 1965:	5019675
June 1965:	5075750
August 1965 (final):	5093413
August 1965 (new system starting, see above):	6101001
January 1966:	6159030

Fig. 7. Victor 101 model FCW Super Estate Car, 1966-67

Fig. 8. Victor 101 Estate Car, interior view showing rear seat folded down

Fig. 9. Victor 101 front door, showing pronounced curvature of
doors and window glass

MODIFICATIONS

NOTE: For modifications of a purely technical nature, see *Repair Data*.

October 1965: 1966 models introduced with minor modifications. On the De Luxe
models (FCE and FCG) walnut veneer is used to improve the appearance of the
facia. On the VX 4/90 the instrument style was changed to white figures on a black
background, instead of black on white. The Super Traction differential, which was
introduced in May 1965 as a production option became standard equipment on
the VX 4/90, continuing as an extra-cost option on Victors. Powerglide automatic
transmission had been introduced as optional extra for all models in June 1965.

As from Engine Number 30FC/100111, the engine was modified in several
respects, resulting in increased output, improved torque and higher mechanical
efficiency. The new bhp figure is 75 (gross) at 4800 rpm, compared with 70 (gross)
at 4800 rpm on earlier models. Gross torque was raised from 94·2 lb ft at 2800 rpm
to 95 at 2600 rpm. The various modifications were as follows:

New carburettor with larger choke tube. New inlet manifold with larger internal passages. Larger and smoother-flow cylinder-head inlet ports. Larger and re-positioned intake tube on air-cleaner. New type cylinder-head gasket. Better crank-case ventilation to reduce oil sludging and prevent crankcase emission. Stronger, more durable piston rings. Redesigned main bearings and main bearing shells. Flexibly mounted flywheel to improve engine smoothness and silence. Heavy-duty exhaust system for longer life and quieter running. From Chassis Number 5047973 the rear brakes are no longer self-adjusting.

On VX 4/90 only:
New cast-iron clutch housing. New type of air-cleaner, incorporating two paper-type elements.

September 1966: 1967 models introduced featuring the following detail improve-ments and modifications. The wide bright metal capping along front wings and waistline was replaced by a narrow beading below the capping, which is now finished in body colour. Victor models fitted with a new anodised aluminium radiator grille. Victor De Luxe fitted with bright sill moulding below the doors and, like the VX 4/90, new wheel trims. Re-designed seating and improved interior trim. Walnut facia and figured walnut panel on transmission tunnel introduced as new extra-luxury features for the VX 4/90. New rear-door weather strip for more efficient sealing. Improved construction of windscreen glass channel to prevent distortion. Shatter-proof internal rear-view mirror. Wax-capsule thermostat for more precise and constant temperature control. Improved synchromesh for longer life. Negative earth electric system to accommodate the alternator, which is now optional equip-ment. Improved brakes with new type of lining material. Bigger front brake cylinders and more efficient non-return valves (Victor only). Larger wheels and tyres (6·50–13) for Estate Cars, optional for all Victor saloons. 'VX 4/90' designation relocated, from rear quarter panels to lower part of rear wings.

PRICES (UK)

Prices are inclusive of purchase tax and to the nearest £1.

	Oct. 1964	May 1965	Oct. 1965	Aug. 1966	Feb. 1967
Victor 101 Saloons:					
FCS (basic):	£678	£690	£690	£702	£702
FCD (Super):	£708	£718	£718	£731	£753
FCE (De Luxe):	£763	£775	£774	£788	£788
Victor 101 Estate Cars:					
FCW (Super):	£775	£793	£793	£807	£829
FCG (De Luxe):	£859	£878	£878	£893	£893
VX 4/90 Saloon:					
FCH:	£872	£884	£893*	£909*	£909*
Optional extras:					
Four-speed gearbox**:	£14½	£14½	£14½	£15	£15
Powerglide automatic transmission:	N.A.	N.A.	£97	£98	£98
Super Traction differential*:	N.A.	£10	£10	£10	£10
Individual front seats (FCS/D/W):	£12	£12	£12	£12	N.A.
Front disc/power brakes**:	£15	£15	£15	£15	£15
Leather upholstery (FCE/G):	£12	£12	£12	£12	£12

*Super Traction differential standard on FCH from October 1965.
**Standard on FCH.

Fig. 10. Victor 101 facia and front compartment (1966 model FCE shown)

INSTRUMENTS AND CONTROLS

Key to Fig. 12
 1 Cigarette lighter (if fitted)
 2 Heater temperature control (if fitted)
 3 Glove compartment lock
 4 Choke control
 5 Ventilation control (if fitted)
 6 Water temperature gauge
 7 Direction indicator warning light (green)
 8 Oil pressure warning light (orange)
 9 Mileage recorder and speedometer
10 Horn ring

11 Fuel gauge
12 Ignition/generator warning light (red)
13 Direction indicator warning light (green)
14 Direction indicator switch lever
15 Windscreen wiper control
16 Fog light switch (if fitted)
17 Light switch
18 Parking brake lever
19 Dip switch
20 Ignition/starter switch
21 Bonnet lock release control

Key to Fig. 13
 1 Direction indicator switch lever
 2 Water temperature gauge
 3 Direction indicator warning light (green)
 4 Oil pressure gauge
 5 Headlight main beam warning light (blue)
 6 Engine rev indicator (tachometer)
 7 Horn ring
 8 Speedometer with mileage total and trip
   recorder
 9 Ignition/generator warning light
10 Ammeter
11 Direction indicator warning light

12 Fuel gauge
13 Heater temperature control
14 Ventilation control
15 Bonnet lock release control
16 Light switch
17 Fog light switch (if fitted)
18 Windscreen wiper control
19 Dip switch
20 Trip recorder re-set control
21 Ignition/starter switch
22 Choke control
23 Cigarette lighter (if fitted)
24 Glove compartment lock

Fig. 11. VX 4/90 facia (1966 model FCH shown)

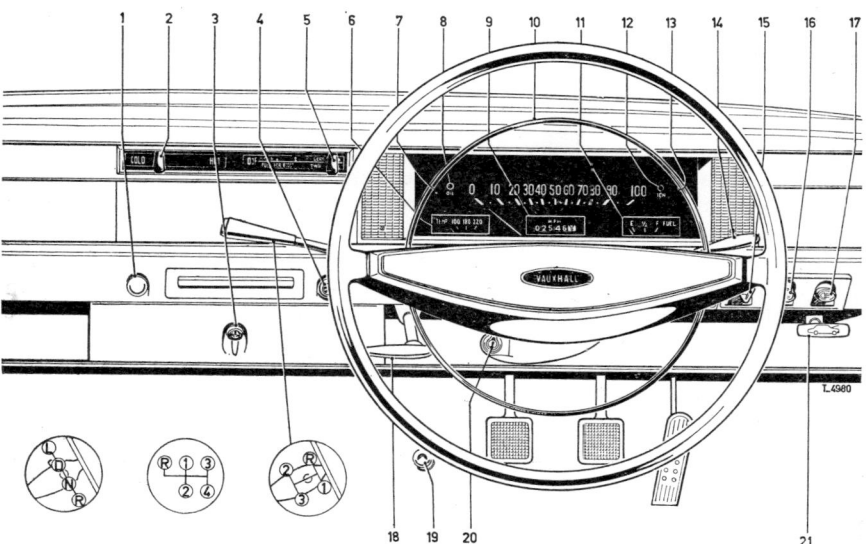

Fig. 12. Instruments and controls, Victor 101 (right-hand drive shown)

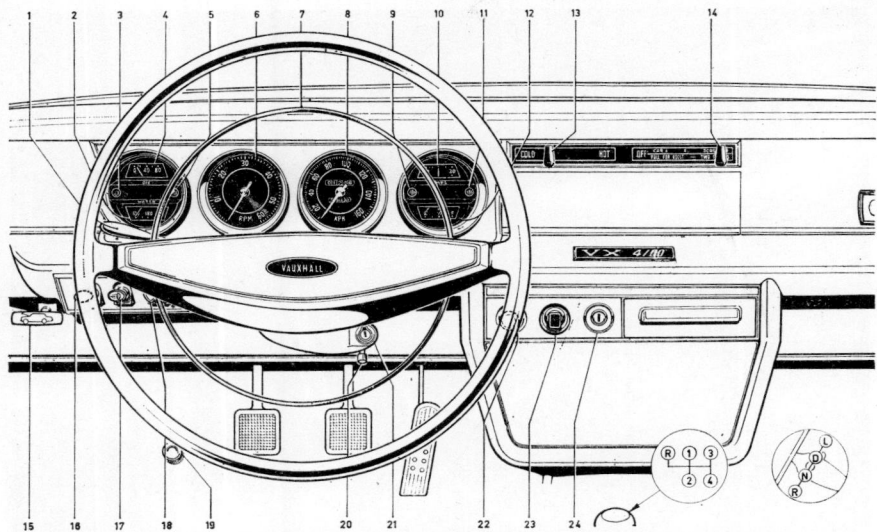

Fig. 13. Instruments and controls, VX 4/90 (left-hand drive shown)

Automatic transmission: The Powerglide automatic transmission, first introduced by Chevrolet in 1949, became available as a production option on the Victor and VX 4/90 models in June 1965 and is similar to that used on the six-cylinder PC (Cresta) models, except for ratios and the omission of the 'P' position. The selector positions are L–D–N–R and the selector lever is mounted on the steering column.

The various positions are briefly explained as follows:

N – *Neutral and starting.* An inhibitor switch is wired in series with the starter solenoid, ensuring that the starter operates only when the selector lever is in this position.

D – *Drive—fully automatic normal forward driving range.* Most driving is done with the selector in this position. After depressing the accelerator pedal the car will move off in the low range and from then on the transmission will select the best ratio as circumstances dictate.

L – *Low range.* Limitation to low range only. The transmission will now not shift up into the high range, thus providing maximum pulling power or, on steep declines, maximum engine braking. The selector lever should be lifted before selecting this position. Low range should not be selected on normal roads at speeds above 45 mph or on slippery or icy roads above 10 mph, otherwise a skid may be induced.

R – *Reverse.* Do not select at speeds above 10 mph.

'*Kick-down.*' In addition to the above selector positions, a detent in the throttle linkage interrupts the pedal travel before full-throttle position. To induce a forced downshift of the transmission, the accelerator pedal must be depressed beyond the detent point. While the pedal is depressed beyond this point, the low ratio will remain engaged up to a higher maximum speed.

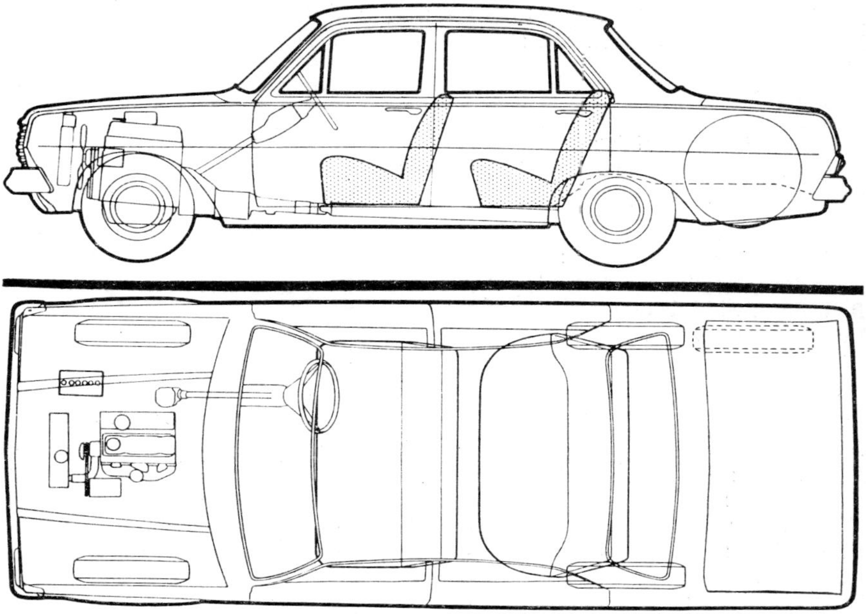

Fig. 14. General arrangement, side elevation and plan view

Dimensions and Weights

EXTERIOR DIMENSIONS

	inches	
Wheelbase:	100·0	8ft 4in
Track, front:	51·0	
Track, rear:	52·6	
Overall length:	174·7	14ft 6in
Overall width:	64·7	5ft 4 7/10in
Overall height:	55·3	
Ground clearance (minimum):	6·0	
Turning circle:	33·0ft	

INTERIOR DIMENSIONS

Pedal to front seat:	13–18
Steering wheel to seat:	5·0
Steering wheel to seat back-rest:	11–16
Height over front seat:	40·0
Height of front seat:	14·0
Depth of front seat:	20·0

Maximum adjustment travel of front seat:	5·0
Front seat back-rest to rear seat:	7–11
Height over rear seat:	38·0
Height of rear seat:	13·0
Depth of rear seat:	18·0
Maximum interior height:	45·0
Height of luggage compartment (maximum):	17·0
Depth of luggage compartment:	47·0

ESTATE CARS, ADDITIONAL DIMENSIONS

Rear floor, maximum length:	69·0
Rear floor, length behind rear seats:	47·7
Rear floor, width between wheel arches:	41·5
Loading space, maximum width:	53·7
Loading space, maximum height:	33·2

WEIGHTS

Model	Shipping weight	Kerb weight	GVW	Axle ratings Front	Rear
FCS Saloon:	2104 lb	2194 lb	3150 lb	1500 lb	1800 lb
FCD Saloon:	2101 lb	2192 lb	3150 lb	1500 lb	1800 lb
FCE Saloon:	2148 lb	2240 lb	3150 lb	1500 lb	1800 lb
FCH Saloon:	2164 lb	2256 lb	3150 lb	1500 lb	1800 lb
FCW Estate Car:	2251 lb	2341 lb	3368 lb	1500 lb	1900 lb
FCG Estate Car:	2277 lb	2369 lb	3368 lb	1500 lb	1900 lb

NOTE: *Shipping weights* are for basic vehicle with all regular equipment but ex-
cluding weight of fuel and water.
Kerb weights are shipping weights plus weight for fuel and water.
GVW is maximum allowable gross vehicle weight.
Axle ratings are individual weights on axles, which must not be exceeded.
Additional information for Estate Cars when towing trailers:

Maximum weight of trailer or caravan:	2240 lb
Maximum download at attachment point:	100 lb
Maximum vehicle weight when towing:	3188 lb
Maximum gradient negotiable with full load:	1:6

Using roof rack: Distributed load on roof must not exceed 100 lb and should be
included when calculating GVW.

Technical Specifications
ENGINE

	Victor up to engine number 30FC/100110	Victor from engine number 30FC/100111	VX 4/90 FCH
Model:	FC 30	FC 30	FC 31
Type:		four-cylinder in-line, four-stroke, water-cooled	
Cylinders:		four	
Valve arrangement:		overhead (pushrod-operated)	
Bore and stroke, inches:		3·214 x 3·000	
mm:		81·64 x 76·20	

Cubic capacity, cubic inches:		97·4	
cc:		1594	
Compression ratio, to 1:	9·0*	9·0*	9·3
Maximum bhp at rpm, gross:	70·0 at 4800	76·0 at 4800	85·5 at 5200
net:	60·3 at 4600	66·0 at 4800	73·8 at 5200
Maximum bmep, lb/sq in at rpm:	133·9 at 2400	138·5 at 2400	143·4 at 2800
Maximum torque, ft lb at rpm,			
gross:	94·2 at 2800	95·0 at 2600	98·7 at 3200
net:	86·3 at 2400	89·0 at 2400	91·8 at 2800
Top gear mph at 1000 rpm:	16·3	16·3	17·2
Carburettor, make and model:		Zenith 34 IV	
number:	one	one	two
*7·0 optional			

TRANSMISSION

Manual Transmission:	*Victor*	*VX*4/90*
Clutch, type:	sdp 8 in	sdp 8 in
make and model:		Borg & Beck 8 A6
Gearbox (manual), type:	3F1R s/m	4F1R s/m
Gear ratios to 1, first gear:	3·186	3·285
second gear:	1·635	2·130
third gear:	—	1·355
top gear:	1·000	1·000
reverse:	3·050	3·050
Final drive, type:		hypoid
gear ratio to 1:	4·125**	3·900
Overall gear ratios to 1, first gear:	13·14	12·83
second gear:	6·74	8·31
third gear:	—	5·29
top gear:	4·125	3·90
reverse:	12·58	11·89

*Four-speed gearbox optional on Victor (code 177), but final drive remains 4·125.
**4·625 to 1 (8/37) available to special order (code 225).

Automatic transmission (optional, code 389):

Make and type:	Powerglide hydraulically-operated compound planetary gear train providing two forward ratios and reverse, coupled to a three-element torque converter (ratio 2.6 : 1).
Control:	selector on steering column (LDNR)
Transmission ratios to 1, low:	1·82 to 4·73
high:	1·00 to 2·6
reverse:	1·82 to 4·73

	Victor	*VX* 4/90
Final drive type and ratio to 1:	hypoid 4·125	hypoid 3·900
Overall ratios to 1, low:	19·511	18·447
high:	10·725	10·140
reverse:	19·511	18·447

CHASSIS

Chassis construction: unitary body-cum-chassis
Suspension, front: independent with wishbones, coil springs
                                              and torsion bar stabiliser
              rear: semi-elliptical leaf springs
Shock-absorbers, front and rear: hydraulic double-acting telescopic
Steering gear, make: Burman or Cam Gears
              type: recirculating ball
              ratio to 1:   15·7 (straight-ahead position)
              wheel diameter: 16·0in
              number of turns: 4·0 (from lock to lock)
Wheels, make and type*:   Sankey, steel disc
              rim size: 4J x 13, well-base
              offset: 1·56in
Tyres, type and size: tubeless
       Saloons, standard: 5·60–13, 4-ply
               optional*:   5·90–13, 4-ply or 155–13 radial
       Estate Cars, standard*:   5·90–13, 6-ply
               optional: 155–13 radial
*From September 1966 oversize wheels and tyres (6.50–13) are standard equipment
on Estate Cars, optional on all saloons.
Brakes, make and type:
       Victor, standard: Girling, 2LS front, L and T rear
               optional: Girling disc front, duo-servo drum rear
       VX 4/90, standard: Girling disc front, duo-servo drum rear
Brake servo assistance (models with
       disc front brakes), make and type: Girling, direct acting vacuum servo
Drum brakes, dimensions:
       drum diameter, front and rear: 9·0in
       total braking swept area: 197 sq in
       lining sizes, front: 7·06 x 1·75in
                   rear, primary: 7·38 x 1·75in
                        secondary: 9·3 x 1·75in
       total lining area (effective):   101·7 sq in
Disc brakes, dimensions*:
       diameter: 9·06in
       thickness: 0·375in
       disc pad friction area: 3·9 sq in (each)
       total braking swept area: 253·1 sq in
       total lining (effective) pad area: 70·3 sq in
*Rear brakes similar to models with four drum brakes.

ELECTRICAL EQUIPMENT

Electrical system: 12 volts
Battery: 12 volts, 38 Ah
Earthing: 1964–66: positive
                                              1966–67: negative
Ignition: coil

THEORETICAL ROAD SPEEDS

(Road speeds in mph, piston speeds in ft/min)

Victor Saloon (manual 4-speed gearbox, 4·125:1 final drive, 5·60–13 tyres):

	rpm	first gear	second gear	third gear	top gear	piston speed
(a)	1000	4·95	7·65	12·00	16·30	500
(b1)	2600	12·78	19·89	31·20	42·38	1300
(b2)	2800	13·86	21·42	33·60	45·64	1400
(c)	4800	23·76	36·72	57·60	78·24	2400

VX 4/90 Saloon (manual gearbox, 3·90:1 final drive, 155–13 tyres):

	rpm	first gear	second gear	third gear	top gear	piston speed
(a)	1000	5·10	7·90	12·40	16·90	500
(b)	3200	16·32	25·28	39·68	54·08	1600
(c)	5200	26·52	40·58	64·48	87·88	2600

(b)=engine speed at maximum torque; for b1 and b2 rpm difference see page 15.
(c)=engine speed at maximum bhp.

PERFORMANCE FIGURES

NOTE: These figures are approximate and should be considered to be fair averages.

(four-speed)	Victor Saloon	VX 4/90	Estate Car
Maximum speed:	85 mph	90 mph	84 mph
Cruising speed:	70 mph	75 mph	70 mph
Cruising range:	275 miles	260 miles	225 miles
Speed in gears (max.), first:	29 mph	30 mph	28 mph
second:	45 mph	47 mph	45 mph
third:	70 mph	74 mph	65 mph
Fuel consumption:	26–29 mpg	24–28 mpg	21–24 mpg

Lubrication and Maintenance

RUNNING-IN PERIOD (first 1000 miles)

During the first 500 miles do not exceed:

with three-speed gearbox:
    50 mph in top gear
    30 mph in second gear
    15 mph in first gear

with four-speed gearbox:
    50 mph in top gear
    35 mph in third gear
    25 mph in second gear
    15 mph in first gear

During the second 500 miles the speeds may be progressively increased. These maximum speeds must not be maintained for long periods. Avoid long periods of idling and avoid over-revving the engine; change down to a lower gear when necessary and avoid fierce acceleration.

GENERAL DATA

Engine: Sump capacity, total: 7½ Imp pints (9 US pints)
          refill: 6 Imp pints (7·2 US pints)
          refill incl. filter: 7 Imp pints (8·4 US pints)

Oil grade: Engine oil MIL–L–2104–A.

Oil viscosities: above 32°C: SAE 30
          32°C to 0°C: SAE 20 or 20W or 20W/30
          0°C to —12°C: SAE 20W or 20W/30
          —12°C to —23°C: SAE 10W
          consistently below —23°C: SAE 5W

Oil dipstick: on right-hand side of cylinder block.
Oil filler cap: on valve rocker cover.
Oil drain plug: at bottom of sump.
Oil drain period: every 6000 miles or three months (whichever occurs first).
Drain oil when the engine is warm.

Crankcase ventilation air-cleaner: wash in petrol or kerosene (paraffin), shake dry and refit, at 12,000-mile or three-monthly intervals, whichever is the earlier.

Oil filter: Partial-flow (by-pass) type on Victor, full-flow type on VX 4/90. Located on left-hand side of engine, below generator. The filter element must be renewed at every engine oil change (6000 miles or three months, whichever is the earlier). Before fitting the new element, clean the filter casing thoroughly and use a new sealing washer.

Filter elements:

    FC 30 engines (Victor):   AC 90, Fram C835PL, Purolator MF.208A
    FC 31 engines (VX 4/90):   AC 73, Fram CH837PL, Purolator M.F222A

Air-cleaner(s): FC 30 (Victor) engine air-cleaners have either a dry paper element or a polyurethane foam element. Both must be cleaned at 6000-mile intervals. With the former type, clean the element by lightly tapping the end surfaces. The element should be renewed every 12,000 miles or six months, which ever is the earlier. With the latter type, which is now obsolete, the element should be washed in kerosene (paraffin), squeezed dry and then re-oiled with engine oil. If excessive oil is accidentally applied, wrap the element in a clean, dry cloth and squeeze out the surplus oil. Never wring or shake the element material. 1964–65 FC 31 (VX/4/90) engines are fitted with twin air-cleaners of the paper element type, which should be serviced as described above. From 1967 a new type of air-cleaner is fitted, incorporating two paper-type elements in one casing.

Cooling system:

Capacities, Victor, without heater:	11¾ Imp pints (14·1 US pints)
Victor, with heater:	13¼ Imp pints (15·9 US pints)
VX 4/90, with heater:	13¼ Imp pints (15·9 US pints)

    The radiator drain-cock is accessible from under the car at the right-hand side. The cylinder block drain-cock is situated on the left-hand side of the engine. Under winter driving conditions, the cooling system must be protected by an anti-freeze solution. Use an ethylene glycol type of anti-freeze. When draining the cooling system, both drain-cocks should be opened and the radiator filler cap removed.

NOTE: If a heater is fitted, the HEAT control lever must be in the HOT position whenever the cooling system is being drained or re-filled. If this is not done, an air-lock may occur. The heater cannot be completely drained and therefore it is necessary to use anti-freeze in winter, rather than draining the system.

Fuel tank: Capacity, all models: 10 Imp gallons (12 US gallons).

Gearbox (manual):

Oil capacity, three-speed:	2·1 Imp pints (2·5 US pints)
four-speed:	2·4 Imp pints (2·9 US pints)
Oil grade and viscosity:	above 0°C Gear Oil SAE 90
	below 0°C Gear Oil SAE 80

Combined oil filler and level plug on the left-hand side of the gearbox.
Oil level check interval: 12,000 miles or six months, whichever occurs first.
Oil change: no periodic oil change is required.
NOTE: If a complete refill is necessary, a straight mineral gear oil SAE 80 should be used. Never use EP oil.

Automatic transmission (Powerglide, if fitted):

Fluid capacity, refill: approx. 4 Imp pints (4·8 US pints)

Recommended lubricant: Automatic Transmission Fluid, ATF Type A, Suffix A (GM Spec. 9985039; Vauxhall Spec. L–53, available from Vauxhall dealers as 'Powerglide Transmission Fluid' in one-gallon tins under part number 7178761.)

Fluid level check interval: every 6000 miles or three months, whichever is the earlier.

Fluid level dipstick: in engine compartment, at the rear, to the right of the engine.

Fluid change interval: every 12,000 miles or six months, whichever occurs first.

NOTE: Utmost cleanliness is essential when checking the fluid level or topping-up. Always clean the filler cap and the top of the filler pipe before removing the cap and the dipstick. Use only nylon rag for cleaning.

Fluid level check procedure:

(1) Stand car on level ground, transmission at normal operating temperature.

(2) Let engine idle and place selector lever in 'N' position. Apply parking brake.

(3) Clean dipstick and filler pipe area with nylon rag and take dipstick reading. An inaccurate reading will be obtained if the level is checked when the transmission is cold.

(4) If the level is low, add sufficient fluid to bring the level to the 'FULL' mark. Use a clean funnel with a fine-mesh gauze filter.

(5) If significant topping-up is required, check for leakage and rectify immediately.

Fluid change procedure:

(1) Stand car on level ground, transmission at normal operating temperature.

NOTE: At this temperature the fluid will be hot enough to cause serious burns to the skin unless suitable precautions are taken.

(2) Remove drain plug at the front of the transmission case sump. The amount of fluid which can be drained off is about four pints (4·8 US pints) since some of the fluid will remain in the torque converter.

(3) After draining, replace the drain plug and add 4 Imp pints (4·8 US pints) of the recommended fluid through the filler pipe.

(4) Run the car until the transmission is at its normal operating temperature, check the fluid level as described above and add fluid as required to adjust to the correct level.

Towing precautions: Towing can be carried out safely at speeds up to 30 mph for distances up to 10 miles with the selector in 'N' position, *provided* that there is nothing wrong with the Powerglide transmission. For longer distances, or if the transmission is out of order or damaged, the propeller shaft must be disconnected before towing commences. Alternatively the car may, of course, be towed with the rear wheels lifted off the ground.

NOTE: Always check the fluid level after the car has been towed, and top-up.

Rear axle/Differential (standard type):

Oil capacity: 2½ Imp pints (3 US pints).

Oil grade and viscosity: MIL–L–2105B, Hypoid Gear oil

above —18°C SAE 90 EP

below —18°C SAE 80 EP

Combined oil filler and level plug at the rear of the differential housing.

Oil level check interval: 12,000 miles or six months, whichever occurs first.

Oil change: no periodic oil change is required.

NOTE: If the axle has to be drained before completing 10,000 miles, or if new hypoid gears have to be fitted, use only Castrol Thio-Hypoy FD for refilling.

Super Traction Differential (if fitted): The Super Traction limited slip differential is fitted as standard on VX 4/90 models from September 1965, and may be fitted as an optional extra on Victors and early VX 4/90 models from May 1965. It can be identified by the letter 'L' stamped adjacent to the ratio marking on the axle housing, and by an aluminium label retained by the axle filler plug.

Oil capacity: 2½ Imp pints (3 US pints).

Oil grade, UK: special 'Hypoid oil (Gulf) Spin Resistant Axle,' available from Vauxhall dealers in 3-pint tins, under part number 7178760.

Overseas: Hypoid gear lubricant VM Spec. L–36/2, type 3, Gulf oil R73–C.

For oil level/filler plug and level check intervals see under standard type rear axle.

Steering gear:

Oil capacity, Burman: 0·44 Imp pint (0·53 US pint)

Cam Gears: 0·69 Imp pint (0·83 US pint)

Oil grade and viscosity: GM 4655–M (MIL–L–2105B) Hypoid gear oil SAE 90.

Oil filler and level plug: in top of steering gear housing.

Oil level check interval: 12,000 miles or six months, whichever occurs first.

Top-up to bottom of filler plug orifice.

Brake system: The brake fluid reservoir is located on the scuttle under the bonnet on the driver's side.

Capacity of master cylinder assembly, Victor: 0·34 Imp pint (0·41 US pint),

VX 4/90 and Victor with optional disc front brakes: 0·50 Imp pint (0·60 US pint).

Recommended fluid: Castrol-Girling Brake and Clutch Fluid (Crimson).

Fluid level check interval: every 6000 miles or three months, whichever is the earlier.

Grease nipples: Four grease nipples, fitted to the front suspension arm ball-joints. Lubricate every 30,000 miles or 15 months (whichever is the earlier) with special grease to GM specification 4530–M (BP Energrease L21M, Castrol Castrolease MS3, Duckham's LBM 10 Grease, Esso MP Grease (Moly), Gulf Gulflex Moly, Petrofina Fina Marson LM2, Regent Grease 904, Shell Retinax A.M.).

Wheel bearings: The front wheel bearings need lubrication every 30,000 miles or 15 months, whichever occurs first. Repack with grease to Vauxhall specification VM Spec. L–42 (VX 4/90 and Victor models with disc front brakes) or VM Spec. L–17/1 (other Victor models). This job requires specialised knowledge and equipment, and it is recommended to have it performed by an authorised dealer.

TYRE PRESSURES

Tyre sizes, Saloons: 5·60–13 or 5·90–13 (optional on later models 6·50–13), tubeless

Estate Cars: 5·90–13, later models 6·50–13, tubeless

Tyre pressures (cold, lb/sq in)*:	*Front*	*Rear*
Victor Saloons, 5·60–13:	24	24
6·50–13:	25	25
VX 4/90 Saloons, 5·60–13:	26**	26**
Estate Cars, 5·90–13:	24	24***
6·50–13:	25	25***

*See tyre manufacturers' instructions for sizes not listed here.

**For lengthy periods at sustained speeds of 85–90 mph the pressures should be 6 lb/sq in above normal; for motoring which is mostly continuous high speeds, specially designed tyres at pressures recommended by the tyre manufacturers should be used.

***When loaded with driver and three passengers; when loaded to a total weight of 3368 lb, increase pressures to 30 lb/sq in.

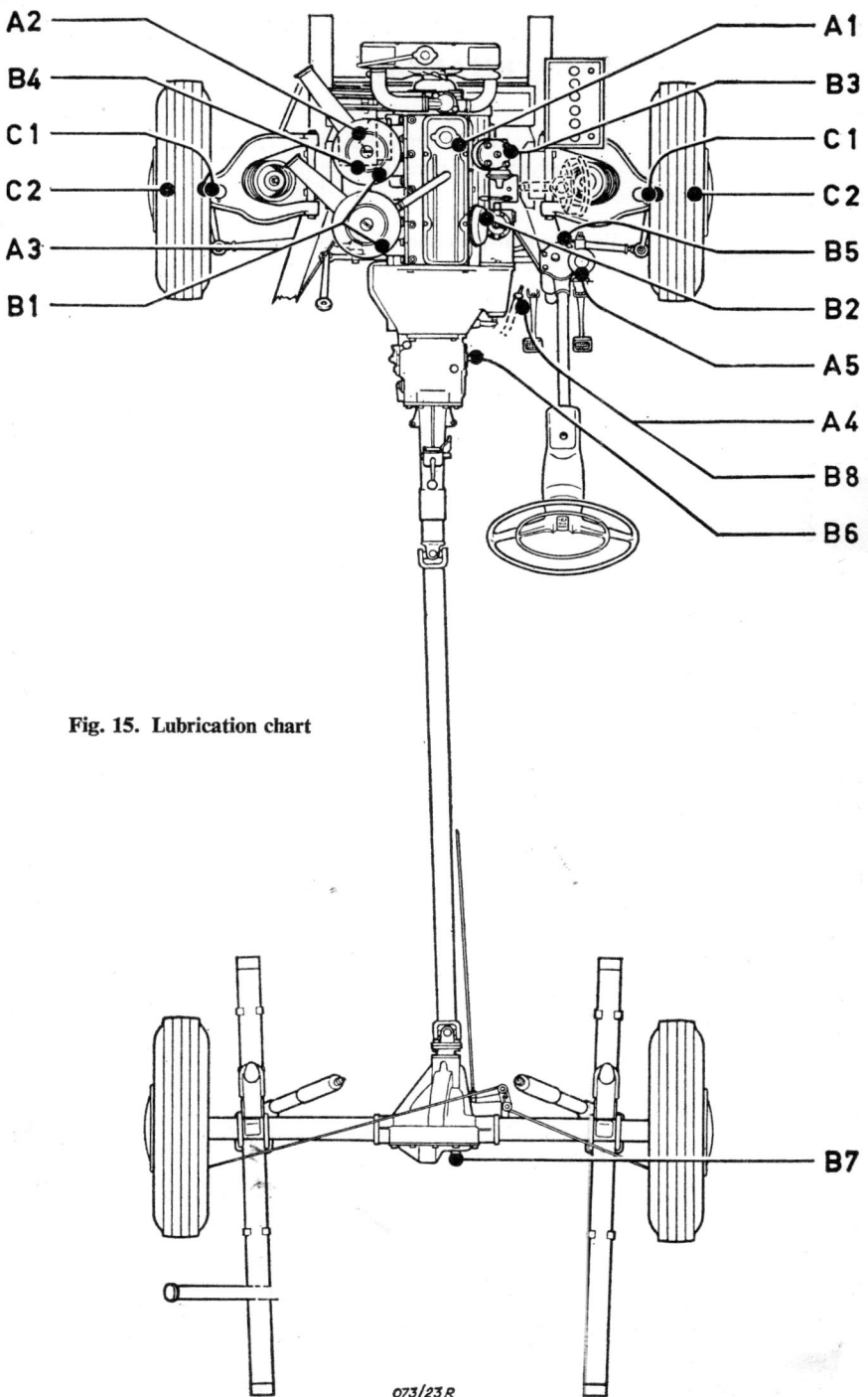

A2

A1

B4

B3

C1

C1

C2

C2

A3

B5

B1

B2

A5

A4

B8

B6

Fig. 15. Lubrication chart

B7

073/23R

ROUTINE MAINTENANCE

Daily: Check engine oil level, cooling system, fuel tank, tyres.
Weekly: Check battery electrolyte, tyre pressures.

A. Every 6000 miles or three months, whichever occurs first:

*A*1 Engine sump: drain (when hot) and refill.

*A*2 Engine oil filter: renew element.

*A*3 Air-cleaner(s) (dry type): clean paper element(s) by gently tapping the end surfaces; clean housing(s).
Air-cleaner (oil-wetted type): wash polyurethane-foam element in paraffin, squeeze dry and re-oil sparingly with engine oil.

*A*4 Automatic transmission (if fitted): check fluid level, top-up if necessary. (See page 19.)

*A*5 Brake fluid reservoir: check fluid level, top-up with brake fluid if necessary.
Throttle, gearshift, clutch and brake linkages: lubricate with engine oil.
Engine: check for oil or water leaks; check fan belt.
Fuel system: check for leaks; clean fuel pump filter.
Ignition system: clean, check and if necessary adjust spark plugs and contact breaker points.
Clutch: check adjustment of free play.
Brake system: check for leaks; check disc brake pads for wear; adjust brakes.
Suspension: check shock-absorbers for leaks.
Electrical: check battery terminals, lights, instruments, heater and accessories.

B. Every 12,000 miles or six months, whichever occurs first:

*B*1 Air-cleaner(s): renew filter element(s) (both types).

*B*2 Engine crankcase breather: remove air-cleaner and wash in petrol or paraffin, shake dry and re-oil element.

*B*3 Ignition distributor: lubricate with a few drops of engine oil on felt pad under rotor, replenish reservoir with a teaspoonful of engine oil through oil-hole, lightly smear cam profile with grease.

*B*4 Dynamo: lubricate rear bearing with a few drops of engine oil.

*B*5 Steering box: check oil level, top-up if necessary.

*B*6 Gearbox: check oil level, top-up if necessary.

*B*7 Rear axle/differential: check oil level, top-up if necessary.

*B*8 Automatic transmission (if fitted): drain and refill. (See page 19.)
Bodywork: lubricate door, bonnet, and boot lid hinges and strikers with a few drops of engine oil.
Brake system: renew servo air-filter on models fitted with front disc brakes; inspect pads and/or linings.
Steering: inspect steering system.

C. Every 30,000 miles or 15 months, whichever occurs first:

*C*1 Front suspension arm ball-joints: lubricate with grease gun (4 nipples); check rubber boots.

*C*2 Front wheel bearings: clean and repack with grease.

Fig. 16. FC30 engine, fitted with (optional) Powerglide transmission

Repair Data

Repairs are best performed by authorized Vauxhall dealers, who possess the necessary experience and special tools. These data were compiled from official workshop manuals and other publications, supplied through the courtesy of Vauxhall Motors Limited, Luton, Beds.

ENGINE

Description:

Engine model, Victor: FC 30, engine number prefix 30FC

         VX 4/90:   FC 31 (twin carburettors), engine number prefix 31FC

Water-cooled, four-cylinder, over-square, four-stroke, in-line petrol engine, with push-rod operated ohv mechanism, built in unit with clutch and gearbox, mounted longitudinally in the front of the vehicle by means of three flexible rubber mountings. The engine can be removed from the vehicle, leaving the gearbox *in situ*.

The pressurized cooling system incorporates a transversely mounted radiator, situated in front of the engine, a thermostat of the bellows-type, an impeller-type water pump with a four-bladed fan driven in tandem with the generator by a V-belt from the crankshaft pulley: V-belt adjustment is obtained in the conventional manner, by loosening the generator mountings and pivoting the generator away from or toward the engine as necessary.

The radiator filler cap incorporates a pressure relief valve which opens when the pressure in the system exceeds 7 lb/sq in. The thermostat is housed in the cooling water outlet pipe flange on the forward end of the cylinder head; it serves to provide quick engine-warm-up when starting from cold and to maintain the requisite engine operating temperature under all conditions.

The chromium cast-iron cylinder head of the FC30 engine is fitted with replaceable shrunk-in valve guides, but the valve seats are machined directly into the cylinder-head material, rendering them non-replaceable.

The aluminium die-cast cylinder head of the FC31 engine has replaceable valve guides which are placed at an angle; the valve seats are pressed-in non-replaceable valve seat inserts.

The valves of both engine types are fitted with single valve springs and are kept in place in the conventional manner by means of semi-circular valve-keepers; the stems of the inlet valves are fitted with O-ring type oil-seals, which prevent oil from entering the combustion chamber by the vacuum created when the piston is on its suction stroke.

The hollow steel valve rocker shaft is attached to the cylinder head by means of four detachable rocker-shaft supports.

The pearlitic malleable cast-iron valve rockers are assembled on the valve rocker shaft, each valve rocker being thrust against its nearest rocker-shaft support by the action of light spacing springs. Each rocker is fitted with a spherical stud with a locking nut to adjust the valve-rocker-to-valve-stem clearance.

The action of the camshaft is transmitted to the valve mechanism by means of solid steel push-rods and chilled cast-iron tappets of the 'barrel' type. The cast-iron camshaft is situated in the right-hand side of the crankcase and runs in three replaceable bearing bushes which are lined with white metal. The camshaft end-thrust is taken by a thrust plate between the timing chain sprocket and No. 1 journal face. The camshaft is driven from the crankshaft by means of an endless Duplex roller chain. The steel camshaft sprocket is secured to the camshaft by means of a heavy central bolt with a special locking plate. The crankshaft chain sprocket is keyed to the crankshaft; its correct lateral position in relation to the camshaft sprocket is obtained by one or more adjustment shims, stacked behind the sprocket. Chain-flutter and vibration is checked by a Reynold's-type hydraulic chain tensioner, which forces a heat-resisting nitrite rubber friction pad against the chain by the action of the engine oil pressure.

The camshaft is provided with a machined helix between No. 1 and No. 2 bearing journals; from this helix, the gear-type oil-pump, mounted in the crankcase and equipped with a corresponding driven gear, is driven in tandem with the ignition distributor.

The full-pressure engine lubrication system comprises the previously described gear-type oil-pump with a built-in pressure relief valve, a wire gauze pick-up strainer in the lower crankcase, a detachable engine oil sump and an externally mounted by-pass oil filter unit. Unlike the FC30 engines, the FC31 engines are equipped with a full-flow type oil filter with a built-in pressure relief valve, which opens to by-pass the flow of excess oil should severe filter element contamination or congestion occur, making normal filtration impossible and causing excessive pressure build-up.

The oil-pump lifts the oil from the sump through the pick-up strainer and forces it directly into the main oil gallery in the cylinder block; on FC31 engines the oil is fed to the full-flow filter, prior to being directed into the main oil gallery. The main oil gallery is a longitudinal drilling in the left-hand side of the cylinder block. From the main oil gallery, cross drillings in the cylinder block guide the oil to the crankshaft main bearings and the camshaft bearings. The crankshaft is drilled in such a manner that Nos. 1 and 4 connecting-rod bearings receive lubrication from Nos. 1 and 3 main bearings respectively, whereas Nos. 1 and 3 connecting-rod bearings are both oil fed from the centre main bearing.

By means of a vertical drilling in the cylinder block and a corresponding drilling in the cylinder head, oil from the camshaft front bearing is fed through a pipe into

Fig. 17. FC31 engine, fitted with (optional) Powerglide transmission
(Note coiled tube fluid cooler for the automatic transmission)

the hollow valve rocker shaft to lubricate the valve mechanism. After lubricating the valve mechanism, the oil drains back into the sump via the push-rod apertures in the cylinder head.

The top of the helical oil-pump driven gear is coupled to the lower end of the ignition distributor by means of a conventional dog arrangement.

The crankshaft is made of EN.18D-type steel and runs in three replaceable bearing shells which are lined with white metal. The crankshaft has four counterweights and is balanced in unit with the flywheel and clutch assembly. The main bearing shells are available in standard and several undersizes. See note in Technical Data on page 86.

Crankshaft end-float is taken at the centre main bearing by means of four semicircular thrust-washers, lined with white-metal; these thrust-washers are available in standard and three oversizes. At its rear end, the crankshaft has a machined flange onto which is bolted the flywheel fitted with a replaceable shrunk-on starter ring gear. The I-beam section connecting rods are heat-treated stampings of carbon manganese steel; at their lower end the rods are attached to the crankshaft connecting-rod bearing journals, or crankpins, by means of replaceable steel-backed bearing shell inserts, lined with aluminium-tin alloy. These bearing shells are available in several undersizes for the FC30 engines; for FC31 engines, refer to the note under Technical Data on page 86.

At their upper ends, the connecting rods are fitted to the pistons by means of a replaceable lead-bronze steel-backed bearing bush and a case-hardened steel piston pin of the fully-floating type which is kept in place by the conventional circlip arrangement.

The solid skirt type pistons are heat-treated aluminium alloy die castings, fitted with two compression rings and one oil control ring, situated above the off-set piston-pin bore.

The chromium-plated, cargraph-treated top compression ring is tapered; the alloy cast-iron second compression ring is an individual centrifugal casting. The alloy cast-iron oil control ring, which is grooved, chamfered and slotted, is an individual centrifugal casting.

FC30 engines are equipped with one single throat downdraught carburettor; the inlet and exhaust manifolds are bolted together providing a 'hot-spot'. A 'hot-spot' raises the temperature of the inlet manifold so that the fuel/air mixture passes into the engine in a pre-heated and therefore more combustible condition; this is advantageous for quick engine warm-up and ensures a more complete combustion, resulting in better performance and reduced fuel consumption.

FC31 engines are equipped with twin single-throat downdraught carburettors, requiring a different manifold arrangement. The inlet manifold of this engine has a built-in water jacket through which the coolant circulates, thereby pre-heating the fuel/air mixture and so providing better performance characteristics.

Fuel from the rear-mounted petrol tank is fed to the carburettor(s) by means of an externally-mounted mechanical fuel pump of the diaphragm type; it is operated by an eccentric on the camshaft, which actuates the spring-loaded fuel pump arm.

Positive engine breathing is obtained by a wire gauze filter built into the oil filler cap on the valve rocker cover, through which fresh air is drawn into the engine. After circulating, the fumes are exhausted via a rubber outlet hose on the valve rocker cover and drawn into the air-cleaner in a continuous cycle.

Removal and installation of the engine:
Drain the cooling system and the engine oil.

Disconnect the battery terminal cables and detach the water hoses at the radiator and the heater unit. Remove the radiator. Remove the nuts securing the engine front mountings to the chassis crossmember; disconnect the fuel feed pipe at the fuel pump and cap the pipe with a tapered plug to prevent ingress of dirt.

Disconnect the starter-motor cable and the wiring at the coil, the oil pressure sender unit and the generator.

Remove the air-cleaner(s) and disconnect the cable and linkage at the carburettor(s).

Drop the exhaust down-pipe at the manifold flange and remove all clutch bell-housing-to-engine securing bolts. Disconnect the clutch-operating push-rod and unhook the retracting spring at the clutch throw-out fork. Take the weight of the engine with a suitable tackle, ensuring that the 'lift' is taken in the vicinity of the oil filler cap on the valve rocker cover. Pull the engine forward and clear of the gearbox main drive shaft after ensuring that all wiring and operating cables, etc., have been disconnected; then carefully hoist and manoeuvre the unit out and clear of the engine compartment.

Installation is a reversal of the removal operation. Adjust the clutch pedal free travel and fill up the cooling system and engine crankcase to the correct level.

Dismantling the engine:
Strip the engine of its auxiliary equipment and remove the valve cover. Disconnect the valve rocker shaft oil supply pipe after removing the circlip. Remove the valve rocker shaft assembly; on FC31 engines take care not to lose the centralizing sleeves beneath the two outer rocker-shaft supports. Remove the circlips and coil springs from the rocker-shaft ends and slide the valve rocker assemblies from the shaft.

Remove the valve push-rods, keeping them in the order of removal to avoid inter-changing during assembly. Remove the engine side cover plate or tappet cover with its gasket and lift out the valve tappets, taking the same precaution as with the push-rods.

Remove the cylinder-head attaching stud nuts and lift off the cylinder head, followed by the cylinder-head gasket, which should be discarded. With the aid of a suitable valve spring compressing tool, remove the semi-circular valve spring keepers, followed by the spring retainers, the valve springs, the O-ring type oil-seals from the inlet valve stems and the valves; be sure to keep the valves in the order of removal to avoid interchanging during assembly.

Remove the water-pump drive pulley and distance piece, and withdraw the crankshaft pulley followed by the timing case cover. Prior to removal, ensure that the chain tensioner is not completely extended, which indicates excessive timing chain or sprocket wear. If such should be the case, renew the timing gear as an assembly. Bend back the tab of the locking plate and remove the camshaft sprocket central securing bolt. With the aid of suitable levers, ease both sprockets from their respective shafts, preventing the chain from binding by excessive movement of one of the sprockets.

Remove the Woodruff keys from the crankshaft and camshaft. Remove the chain tensioner, the adjustment bolt and the three sealing rings. Remove the timing gear case from the cylinder block.

Remove the engine sump with gasket and remove the oil-pump securing bolt. Disconnect the pump pressure pipe at the crankcase and remove the assembly from the engine.

On FC31 engines remove the oil filter before disconnecting the oil-pump pressure pipe, and remove the assembly from the engine.

Gradually slacken the clutch coverplate-to-flywheel bolts and remove the assembly, taking care not to lose the dowels.

Remove the flywheel-to-crankshaft attaching bolts and withdraw the flywheel.

Mark the piston and connecting-rod assemblies, showing the cylinder bore number from which they are to be removed. The connecting rods and bearing caps are marked during production in order to avoid interchanging of bearing caps.

Remove the connecting-rod bearing caps and bearing shells, and push the piston and connecting-rod assemblies upward and out of the cylinder bores.

NOTE: *When the bearing shells are to be used again, it is of paramount importance that they are kept with their respective bearing caps and connecting rods.*

Mark the position of the crankshaft main bearing caps in relation to the cylinder block and remove the caps with the bearing shells and the two lower semi-circular thrust-washers.

Carefully lift the crankshaft out of the crankcase and remove the main bearing upper half-shells from the block. Be sure to keep the bearing shells in such a manner that they can be replaced in their original positions.

Thoroughly clean and inspect all parts and renew those that are damaged or worn. Renew all joint gaskets and preferably the oil-seals. When cleaning the clutch assembly, do not use solvent of any kind on the clutch driven plate as serious clutch trouble will result.

Assembling the engine:

With the aid of mandrel Z8388, insert new sealing strips into the groove at the rear main bearing and into the groove in the bearing cap. Cut excessive material flush with the crankcase whilst firmly pressing down the mandrel. Liberally lubricate the

C

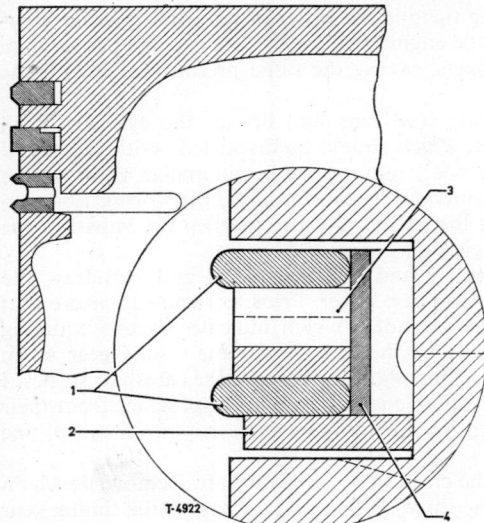

1 Oil control rings
2 Insert
3 Spacer
4 Expander ring

**Fig. 18. Piston rings; inset
shows special service VM oil
control ring components**

sealing strips with engine oil and fit the main bearing upper half-shells to their
respective half-bores in the crankcase. Coat the bearing shells with clean engine oil
and carefully lower the crankshaft into position; locate the crankshaft endwise so
that the upper semi-circular thrust-washers can be fed into the grooves on both
sides of the centre main bearing. The grooved face of each thrust-washer should
face towards the adjacent crankshaft thrust face.

Install the main bearing lower half-shells into the respective bearing caps and
stick the lower semi-circular thrust-washers to both sides of the centre main bearing
cap with a smear of stiff grease. Liberally coat the bearing-cap assemblies with
engine oil, leaving the attaching bolts slack at this stage.

Before tightening the centre main bearing cap bolts, thrust the crankshaft forward
until it contacts the rear upper half thrust-washer; holding the crankshaft in this
position, slide the centre main bearing cap rearwards as far as it will go and tighten
the bearing cap bolts to a torque of 58 lb ft. Using a straight-edge, align the front
face of the front main bearing cap with the front face of the crankcase; tighten the
bearing cap bolts to a torque of 58 lb ft. and re-check the alignment. Adjust as
necessary. Install a dial indicator and measure the crankshaft end-float.

The end-float should be between 0·002–0·004 in. Oversize thrust-washers are
available to correct excessive end-float.

Install the front and main bearing cap oil-seal strips into the grooves between the
sides of each bearing cap and the crankcase. For each groove approximately six
felts are required. Ensure that the strips are firmly packed and that approximately
0·06 in stands proud of the crankcase to oil sump mating face.

Immerse the pistons in hot water to a temperature of 50°C (122°F), lubricate the
piston pin and insert the correct connecting-rod small-end into the piston in such
a manner that the oil-hole in the connecting rod is towards the right-hand side of
the cylinder block when the arrow on the piston top is towards the front; fit the
piston pin and circlips. Measure the piston ring gap of all piston rings in their
respective cylinder bores by inserting each ring squarely a few inches down the
cylinder bore with the aid of an inverted piston. The ring gap thus obtained should

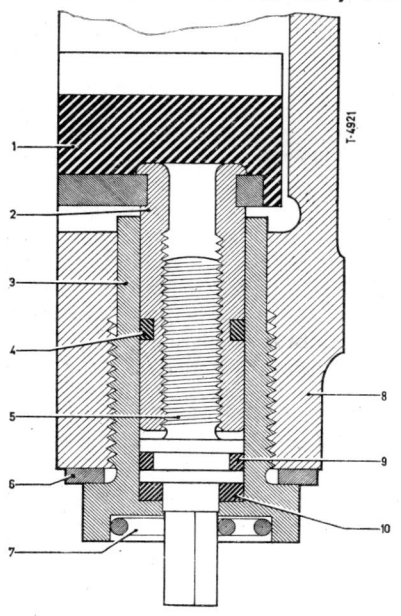

1 Tensioner pad
2 Sleeve
3 Tensioner body
4 Sealing ring
5 Adjusting screw
6 Gasket
7 Circlip
8 Timing chain
9 ⎫
10 ⎬ Seal
   ⎭

Fig. 19. Timing chain tensioner, longitudinal section

amount to 0·008–0·022in for each ring.

Install the piston rings in their respective grooves, paying particular attention to the etched indications 'TOP' and 'BOTTOM'.

Measure the piston ring in groove clearance with the aid of feeler gauges. For tolerances refer to Technical Data.

Liberally lubricate the pistons and piston rings with clean engine oil and divide the piston ring gaps equally around the circumference of the piston, ensure, however, that the oil control ring gap is facing away from the camshaft side of the engine. Install new connecting-rod bolts and with the aid of a suitable piston installing tool insert the piston and connecting-rod assemblies into their appropriate cylinder bores ensuring that the arrows on the piston tops are pointing toward the front of the engine.

NOTE: *When excessive oil consumption is evident, it may be remedied by installing the special service Vauxhall oil control ring set, comprising two steel rails, a spacer, an insert and a corrugated expander ring. When installing this set, be sure to align the rail gap with that of the spacer.*

Install new connecting-rod bearing cap bolts; install the connecting-rod upper half bearing shells into the appropriate connecting rods, liberally lubricate the bearing shells as well as the meticulously-cleaned crankpins and push the pistons further down into the cylinder bores whilst guiding the connecting rods to seat onto the crankpins. Install the connecting-rod lower bearing shells into their respective bearing caps and lubricate with engine oil.

Fit the bearing caps on the respective connecting-rod assemblies and tighten the attaching nuts to a torque of 22lb ft. Ensure that the crankshaft assembly rotates freely. Install the oil-pump and the pick-up strainer.

On FC31 engines use a new sealing washer between the elbow piece of the oil pipe and the crankcase, as well as between the crankcase and the attaching nut.

On FC31 engines, install the oil-filter head with a new sealing washer and locking plate, and secure the bolt.

Install the timing gear casing with a new gasket, which should be coated with sealing compound on both sides.

Liberally lubricate the camshaft bearing journals with engine oil; install a new gasket behind the camshaft thrust flange and carefully insert the camshaft into the bores, taking care not to damage the camshaft bearings.

Install new sealing rings on the chain tensioner pad sleeve and the adjusting collar; smear the gasket and the thread of the tensioner body with sealing compound and assemble the body to the timing casing. Install the pad and the adjusting collar assembly. The pad sleeve must be lubricated and must slide freely in the body bore. Fit the Woodruff keys into the slots in the crankshaft and camshaft; temporarily install both sprockets, less the chain, and turn both shafts so that the scribe-lines on the sprockets are facing each other whilst coinciding with the common centre-line of both sprockets. When in this position, remove both sprockets, taking care not to alter their relative positions; place both sprockets into the chain and then fit the assembly onto the shafts. Once installed, make sure that the scribe-lines are actually positioned as described above.

Having first checked the camshaft end-float with the aid of feeler gauges, secure the camshaft sprocket, using a new locking plate, the tab of which should be bent into one of the sprocket apertures.

Coat the thread of the oil-pump locking bolt with sealing compound; install the pump (see page 33), fit the bolt and tighten the locknut.

Install the engine sump using a new gasket, preferably coated with sealing compound.

Coat both sides of a new timing cover gasket with sealing compound and install the cover. If the crankshaft front oil-seal needs replacing, be sure to install the new seal with its lip facing towards the crankshaft sprocket. It is important to centralize the oil-seal on the crankshaft pulley hub as follows:

Lubricate the crankshaft pulley boss and insert it into the oil-seal with a turning movement to prevent damage to the oil-seal; then install the assembly and secure the cover with the bolts and stud nuts. Secure the crankshaft pulley with the central bolt.

Insert the valves, having first lubricated the valve stems, into the relative valve guides and fit new oil-seals to the inlet valve stems. NOTE: As from engine Nos. 30FC/143124 and 31FC/396642 the intake valve oil-seals and oil-seal groove in the valve stems were deleted. Install the valve springs, valve spring seating washers and valve-keepers with the aid of a suitable valve spring compressing tool. Place a new cylinder-head gasket, coated on both sides with sealing compound, over the cylinder-head attaching studs so that its identification tab is positioned at the left-hand rear end (FC31) or right-hand rear end (FC30) of the cylinder block. Carefully lower the cylinder head onto the cylinder block, fit the plain washers and the stud nuts, which should be tightened to a torque of 73 lb ft in the sequence given below:

10	4	2	6	8	
					front
7	5	1	3	9	

Re-conditioning and checking individual engine components:

Cylinder head: Before reconditioning a cylinder head it is imperative to ensure that the maximum permissible mating face distortion is not exceeded; for both engine types this should not be in excess of 0·005 in, measured lengthwise, and 0·003 in measured across. After planing or re-machining the cylinder-head mating face, the minimum permissible cylinder-head height amounts to 3·282in (FC30 model) or 3·765in (FC31 model).

Assemble the valve spring retainer, spring cap and split collars to each (new) valve in turn and, pulling the valve firmly against its seat, measure the distance between the retainer and the underside of the spring cap. This distance should not exceed 1·54in (FC30 engines) or 1·63in (FC31 engines). If it does exceed this distance the valve seating is too deep in the cylinder head to permit further re-facing and the head must be renewed. NOTE: As from engine Nos. 30FC/149960 and 31FC/13691, a new type of valve spring retainer is fitted, featuring a spring locating lip around the outer edge.

Ensure that the valve stem to valve guide clearance is within the limits of 0·005in on FC30 engines and 0·004in on FC31 engines; if necessary, replace the valve guides as follows:

Valve guides:

*FC*30 *engines:* Remove the old valve guides with service tools Z.8323, and with the aid of tool Z.8243 push the new guides into the bores until the installing tool seats on the cylinder head; this ensures the correct valve guide height above the cylinder head. If this special tool should not be available, make sure that on FC30 engines the valve guide height above the cylinder head amounts to 0·58in.

*FC*31 *engines:* To remove the valve guides on FC31 engines, use the same tool as used on FC30 engines. Place the cylinder head on a drilling machine so that the valve guide to be removed is accurately aligned with the drill-bit. Using a ½in diameter drill-bit, drill out the valve guides to 0·30in from their lower ends; from the combustion chamber press out the remaining parts of the valve guides. Ensure that the bores are perfectly clean and show no burrs or ridges, and with the aid of tool Z.8522 press in the new valve guides, having coated their exteriors thoroughly with engine oil.

Observe the markings on the tool: 'in' for inlet and 'ex' for exhaust valve guides. If these markings are not present, be sure that the inlet valve guides protrude 0·50in and the exhaust valve guides protrude 0·34in from the cylinder head.

After pressing-in new valve guides, the valve seats should be re-machined to be centralized in relation to the new guides. The seat angle should be 45°.

When carrying out this operation, make sure that the valve spring retainer to cylinder head height, as detailed above, is not exceeded. The valve face of used valves should be reground to an angle of 44° and afterwards lapped-in on the appropriate valve seat with a suitable valve grinding compound. Before assembling, be sure to remove all traces of swarf and grinding compound.

NOTE: *All valves of FC31 engines, as well as the exhaust valves of FC30 engines, have aluminized valve seats; this layer may be recognized by a dull glaze; new valves must not be ground or lapped but should be installed in this condition.*

Connecting rods: Fit the connecting-rod bearing caps without the bearing shells and tighten the oiled attaching bolts to 22lb ft; measure the ground bore in rod diameter, which should be 1·9945–1·9950in. Check that the piston pin is an easy sliding fit in the small-end bush; if necessary, install a new bearing bush, ensuring that its oil-hole coincides with that in the rod.

After pressing in the new bush it should be reamed to finishing size, providing an easy sliding fit on the piston pin. Bent or twisted connecting rods may be straightened on a special rod alignment rig.

Crankshaft: Place the crankshaft in V-blocks and carefully check for possible

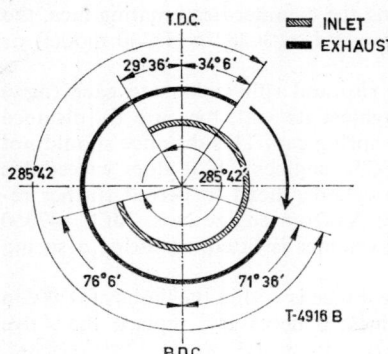

Fig. 20. Valve timing diagram, FC30 and FC31 engines

ovality of the bearing journals. Maximum permissible run-out is $0 \cdot 0015$ in. Check the radial bearing clearance using 'Plastigage' type P.G.1, manufactured by Perfect Circle Corp., Hagerstown, Ind., USA. For clearances and tolerances, refer to Technical Data (page 86). A crankshaft of the FC30 engine may be re-ground to suit one of the undersize bearings as specified in Technical Data.

NOTE : *No regrind specifications for crankshafts of FC31 engines are given as all bearing journals are hardened by a special 'rolling' process. If necessary, install a factory reground exchange crankshaft.*

The production crankshafts of FC30 engines are classified in three tolerance gradings, which can be identified by the letters P, J or PJ.

Crankshafts of grade 'P' are marked with red paint and have a crankpin diameter which differs slightly from the nominal size. Crankshafts of grade 'J' are marked with yellow paint and have a main bearing journal diameter which differs from the nominal size. Crankshafts marked with 'PJ' have main bearing journals as well as crankpin diameters, which differ from the nominal size. The bearing shells are marked with corresponding identification marks.

Replacement crankshafts are available in the standard size only. For specifications refer to Technical Data.

Flywheel and starter ring gear: Check the flywheel locating dowels for wear and ensure that the bolt holes have not become elongated by a possible loose flywheel-to-crankshaft attachment. If necessary, remove burrs and ridges. The shrunk-on starter ring gear can be removed by tapping it off the flywheel in several places around its circumference. Heat the new ring gear until it assumes a dark blue colour, and maintain this temperature for approximately five minutes without exceeding this temperature range, otherwise the temper of the steel will be adversely affected; then quickly tap the heated ring gear onto its seating on the flywheel, the chamfer of the teeth should be facing towards the clutch. If scored or otherwise damaged, the clutch face of the flywheel may be re-machined. If the distance between the clutch face and the front mating face of the flywheel is less than the minimum permissible value of $0 \cdot 490$ in, the flywheel must be replaced.

Camshaft: Carefully examine the camshaft and bearing bushes for wear or damage; if necessary replace the bearings as follows:

With the aid of suitable pilots, remove the bearings, starting with the front bearing, then the centre bearing and finally the rearmost bearing bush, for which it will also be necessary to remove the core plug. The new bearing bushes are then driven in, starting from the rear. Be sure that the notch in the front and rear bearing bush is facing towards the rear of the engine whilst being located in the uppermost position; this ensures correct alignment of the oil-holes in the bushes with the oil drillings in the crankcase.

The camshaft centre bush is not provided with an alignment notch; upon installation be sure to align the oil-hole in the bush with the oil passage to the valve rocker shaft, when the larger oil-hole should coincide with the oil drilling to the centre main bearing. The front of the front bearing must be flush with the front face of the crankcase. Install a new core plug, treated with jointing compound.

Valve timing diagram: The valve timing diagram is checked with the valve rockers adjusted to normal operation clearance. See Fig. 20.

Oil pump: If the oil pump should be removed separately, the engine should be rotated until the rotor arm of the ignition distributor is pointing towards the spark plug segment for No. 1 cylinder and the steel timing ball on the flywheel is positioned exactly in the centre of the inspection hole; this procedure ensures that when installing the oil pump, the ignition timing is not disturbed.

Remove the distributor and the engine sump.

Loosen the oil pump retaining screw locknut and unscrew the retaining screw to release the oil pump.

On FC30 engines, unscrew the oil feed pipe union from the crankcase and lower the oil pump.

On FC31 engines, remove the oil filter and adaptor to gain access for removal of the oil pump feed pipe and elbow assembly. Withdraw the pump. For oil pump clearances and tolerances refer to Technical Data.

Installation is a reversal of the removal operations (also refer to 'assembling the engine' on page 30). Providing the engine has not been rotated, the oil pump is correctly installed when the distributor drive dogs are at right-angles with the camshaft axis and offset towards the rear of the engine.

Static ignition timing: In case the crankshaft has been rotated with the distributor removed from the engine, the initial static ignition setting should be carried out as follows:

Remove the timing hole cover and rotate the crankshaft until the steel ball in the flywheel is exactly in line with the centre of the timing hole notch, at the end of the compression stroke of No. 1 piston. The steel ball indicates 9° BTDC. Make sure that the oil pump gear dogs, visible through the distributor drive shaft aperture, are at right-angles to the camshaft and offset to the rear.

NOTE: Do not attempt to turn the crankshaft by rotating the fan.

Line-up the slots in the distributor shaft with the dogs on the oil pump gear and install the distributor. Slacken the clamp plate nut and secure the clamp plate to the crankcase. Turn the distributor clockwise until the breaker points just start to open, then tighten the clamp plate nut. Check the breaker point gap and adjust if necessary ($0 \cdot 021$–$0 \cdot 023$ for a new, $0 \cdot 019$–$0 \cdot 021$ for a used set of points). Connect a neon timing lamp with its lead to No. 1 spark plug.

On FC30 engines run the engine at normal idling speed, on FC31 engines reduce idling speed to a minimum—this to ensure that the centrifugal advance mechanism does not operate. Direct the light of the timing lamp into the timing aperture; if the timing is correct, the steel ball will be in line with the notch when the lamp flashes. If not, turn the distributor clockwise to advance or anti-clockwise to retard the timing. Recheck the timing after tightening the distributor clamp bolt and on FC31 engines reset the idling speed.

Fuel system: FC30 engines are fitted with one single-throat Zenith-type 34 IV carburettor. Starting from engine number 30FC/00111 this carburettor is fitted with a larger choke-tube, revised jets and an emulsion block discharge tube (auxiliary venturi) that protrudes into the inner venturi.

FC31 engines are equipped with twin Zenith-type 34 IV carburettors.

Idle adjustment, FC30 type engines: Warm-up the engine and turn the idle mixture adjustment screw so that the fastest and most regular engine idling is obtained;

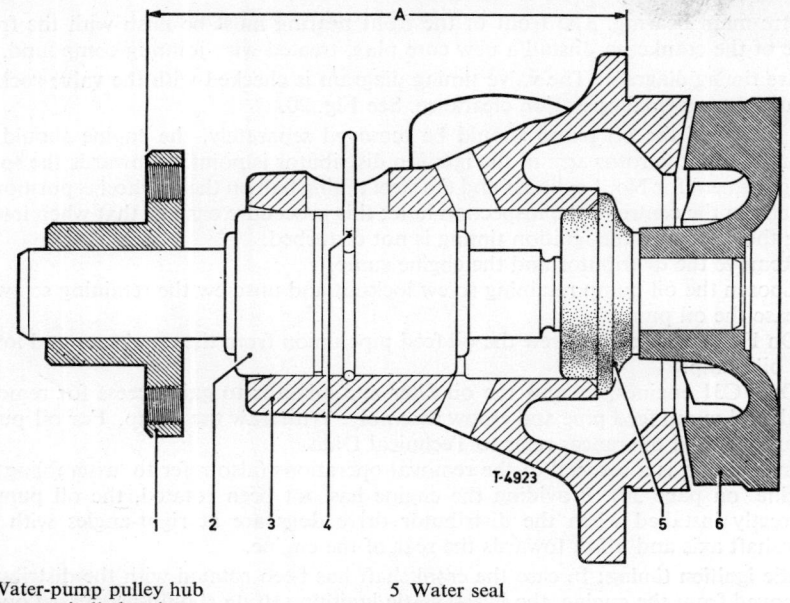

1 Water-pump pulley hub   5 Water seal
2 Pump spindle bearing   6 Impeller
3 Water-pump body   A 3.32 in
4 Snap ring

Fig. 21. Water pump, longitudinal section

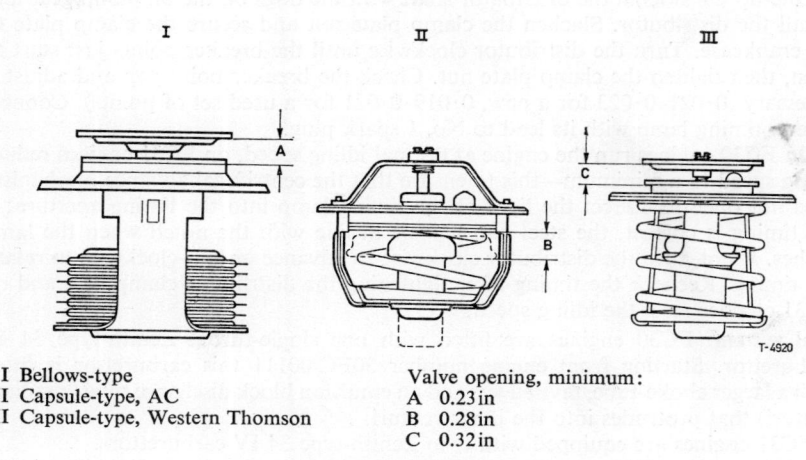

  I Bellows-type   Valve opening, minimum:
 II Capsule-type, AC   A 0.23 in
III Capsule-type, Western Thomson   B 0.28 in
                               C 0.32 in

Fig. 22. Thermostat types

then turn the screw another one-eighth of a turn anti-clockwise to assist starting from cold.

Normally the idle mixture adjustment screw should be turned $1\frac{1}{2}$ turns in an anti-clockwise direction, starting from the fully closed position.

Back-off the throttle stop screw until the engine idles at 550–600 rpm. Depress the accelerator pedal and quickly release to be sure of proper adjustment; should the engine stall, the idle mixture screw should be screwed in by half a turn at a time until the desired result is obtained. If necessary, re-adjust the idling speed with the throttle stop screw.

'Economiser Fix' for early Victors:

If low fuel economy occurs on a Victor 101 (FC30) prior to engine number 30FC/ 99924, Vauxhall dealers can carry out a simple 'Service Fix,' involving revised jetting and the replacement of the paper element type air-cleaner with a wire-mesh type.

Choke valve synchronization on FC31 engines: Remove the air-cleaners from both carburettors. Disconnect the choke cable and loosen the choke valve shaft coupling. Fully close both choke valves and reconnect the shaft coupling as well as the choke cable. Operate the choke control and check that both valves are operated simultaneously. Refit the air-cleaners.

Throttle synchronization and idle speed adjustment on FC31 engines: Warm-up the engine, remove both air-cleaners and disconnect the throttle control rod at the rear carburettor. Loosen the throttle shaft coupling, allowing the front throttle shaft to turn freely in the coupling sleeve; if necessary, align both carburettors to achieve this.

Fully back-off both throttle stop screws and insert a 0·003 in feeler gauge blade between the stop screw and the front carburettor throttle stop; keep the throttle fully closed and turn the stop screw so that its tip just contacts the feeler gauge blade and then an additional $1\frac{1}{2}$ turns farther. Repeat this with the rear carburettor, which will provide a preliminary carburettor synchronization. Fully screw in both idle mixture adjusting screws by hand, then back-off each screw $1\frac{1}{4}$ turns. With the engine at normal operating temperature, adjust the mixture adjusting screw of the front carburettor so that the engine runs regularly. Repeat this with the rear carburettor. Screwing in provides a leaner mixture, screwing out enriches the fuel mixture. Now turn both mixture adjusting screws so that with a vacuum meter connected to the windshield-washer/brake servo unit connection on the inlet manifold, an optimum vacuum reading is indicated (approximately 20 in Hg).

The idling speed should be between 700–750 rpm. Final throttle synchronization should be carried out with the aid of a 'Unisyn' synchronizing device. Upon completion do not forget to retighten the throttle-shaft coupling and to reconnect the hoses and linkages.

Accelerator pump stroke adjustment:

The lower end of the pump operating lever has two holes which connect the operating rod. A longer stroke and thus greater fuel delivery is obtained when connecting the operating rod to the upper hole; the opposite results when engaging the rod with the lower hole in the lever.

For cold season operation the long stroke should be used; for summer time the short stroke suffices.

Water pump: After removal, the water pump is dismantled and reassembled as follows:

With the aid of a suitable extractor, withdraw the pump impeller from the pump spindle and remove the sealing ring.

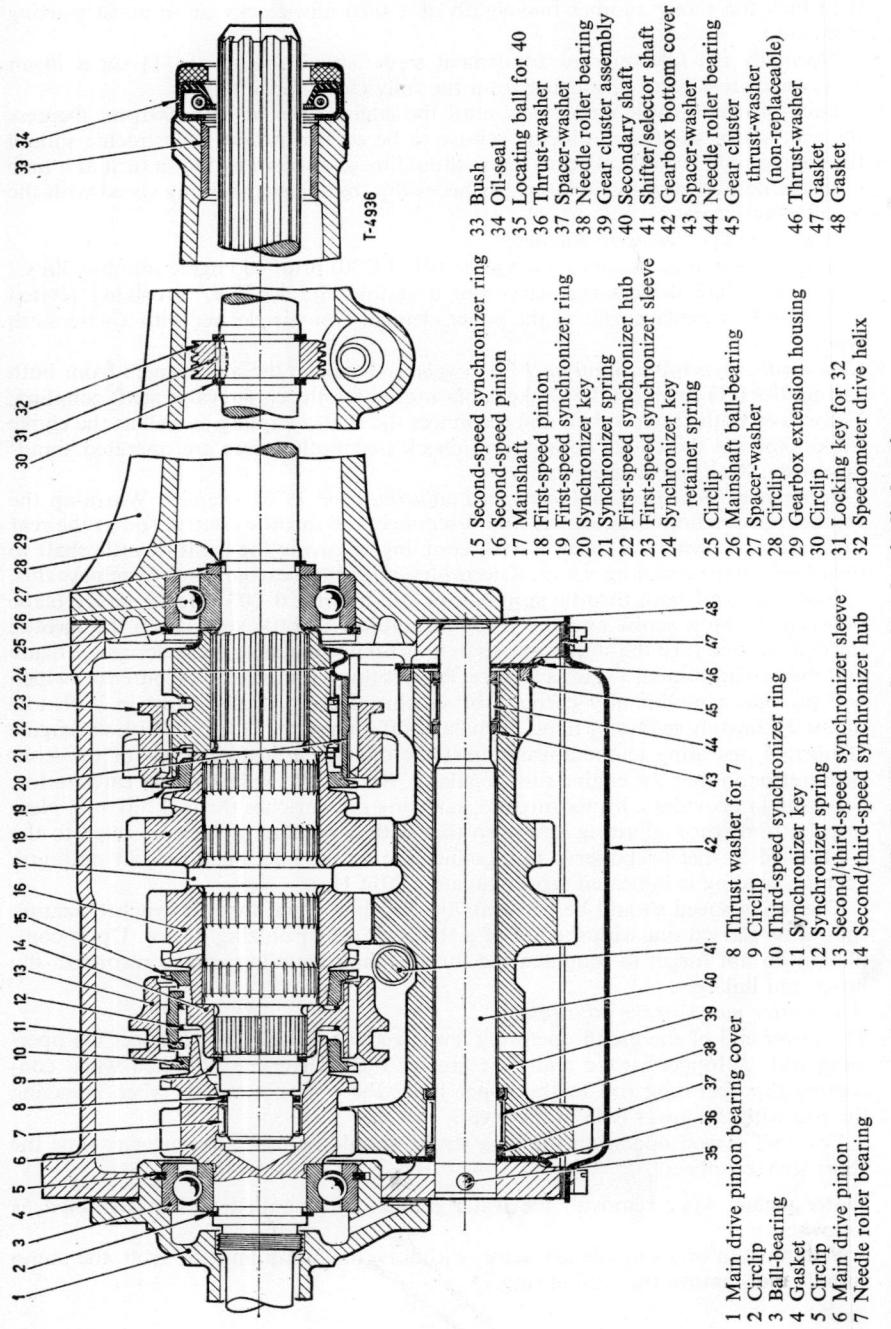

T-4936

1 Main drive pinion bearing cover
2 Circlip
3 Ball-bearing
4 Gasket
5 Circlip
6 Main drive pinion
7 Needle roller bearing
8 Thrust washer for 7
9 Circlip
10 Third-speed synchronizer ring
11 Synchronizer key
12 Synchronizer spring
13 Second/third-speed synchronizer sleeve
14 Second/third-speed synchronizer hub
15 Second-speed synchronizer ring
16 Second-speed pinion
17 Mainshaft
18 First-speed pinion
19 First-speed synchronizer ring
20 Synchronizer key
21 Synchronizer spring
22 First-speed synchronizer hub
23 First-speed synchronizer sleeve
24 Synchronizer key retainer spring
25 Circlip
26 Mainshaft ball-bearing
27 Spacer-washer
28 Circlip
29 Gearbox extension housing
30 Circlip
31 Locking key for 32
32 Speedometer drive helix
33 Bush
34 Oil-seal
35 Locating ball for 40
36 Thrust-washer
37 Spacer-washer
38 Needle roller bearing
39 Gear cluster assembly
40 Secondary shaft
41 Shifter/selector shaft
42 Gearbox bottom cover
43 Spacer-washer
44 Needle roller bearing
45 Gear cluster thrust-washer (non-replaceable)
46 Thrust-washer
47 Gasket
48 Gasket

Fig. 23. Three-speed gearbox, longitudinal section

Examine the pump spindle and the bearing; if necessary, remove the bearing circlip from the pump housing, heat the pump housing in water to 80°C and remove the spindle and bearing.

Press the new spindle, together with the bearing, into the pump housing until the rearmost groove in the bearing coincides with the groove in the pump housing. Secure the bearing with the circlip.

Press a new pulley flange on to the pump spindle until the distance between the front mounting face of the pulley flange and the pump-housing mounting face amounts to 3·32in. Coat a new sealing ring with water pump grease and install with the sealing face towards the impeller into the pump housing.

TRANSMISSION

Clutch: Borg & Beck model 8A6 mechanically-operated single dry plate clutch with six damper springs. Before removing the clutch assembly, make suitable markings on the clutch cover in relation to the flywheel to ensure correct assembly. When installing, the clutch driven plate should be accurately centralized, this can be done with an old gearbox main drive shaft.

The clutch throw-out bearing is grease-packed in production; when servicing the clutch do not wash-out or clean the bearing in solvent.

For data concerning re-machining of the clutch pressure plate and other information, refer to Technical Data.

Clutch pedal free travel adjustment: The clutch pedal free play is measured between the adjusting nut and the clutch operating lever and should amount to 0·10in. Turn the adjusting nut until the requisite free travel is obtained and secure with the locknut. Recheck the pedal free travel and adjust as necessary.

Gearbox: Victor 101 models are equipped with a three- or four-speed gearbox; the VX 4/90 models all have a four-speed gearbox. The four-speed gearboxes are operated by a floor-mounted gear-shift lever, the three-speed gearboxes are operated by means of a steering column mounted gear-shift lever. All forward gears on both gearbox types are synchronized.

Gearbox removal and installation: On cars fitted with a four-speed gearbox, detach the gearshift lever dust boot from the floor. Remove the gearshift lever pivot pin and related parts, and remove the lever proper, the spring and the spring retainer.

Place the rear end of the vehicle on chassis stands and drain the oil from the gearbox. On three-speed models disconnect the gearshift cross-shaft at the shifter/selector shaft and remove the gearbox housing support bracket. Disconnect the propshaft at the pinion flange and remove the assembly from under the car. Disconnect the speedometer drive cable and support the engine. Remove the central nut and washers from the gearbox mounting rubber; remove the four bolts securing the gearbox mounting crossmember and detach the clutch bell housing bottom cover. Detach the gearbox from the clutch bell housing and remove from under the vehicle.

Installation is a direct reversal of the removal operation; paying attention to the following points:

Inspect the clutch throw-out bearing for wear or damage. Lubricate the main drive shaft splines with grease. Fit new lock-washers behind all gearbox mounting bolts and check the three-speed gearshift linkage for correct operation. Refill the gearbox with the recommended lubricant. After driving the vehicle for some distance, recheck the oil level as some oil will have lodged in the gearbox extension housing.

Three- and four-speed gearbox, dismantling: On four-speed gearboxes remove the gearshift linkage. Attach a suitable support plate to the gearbox housing and clamp

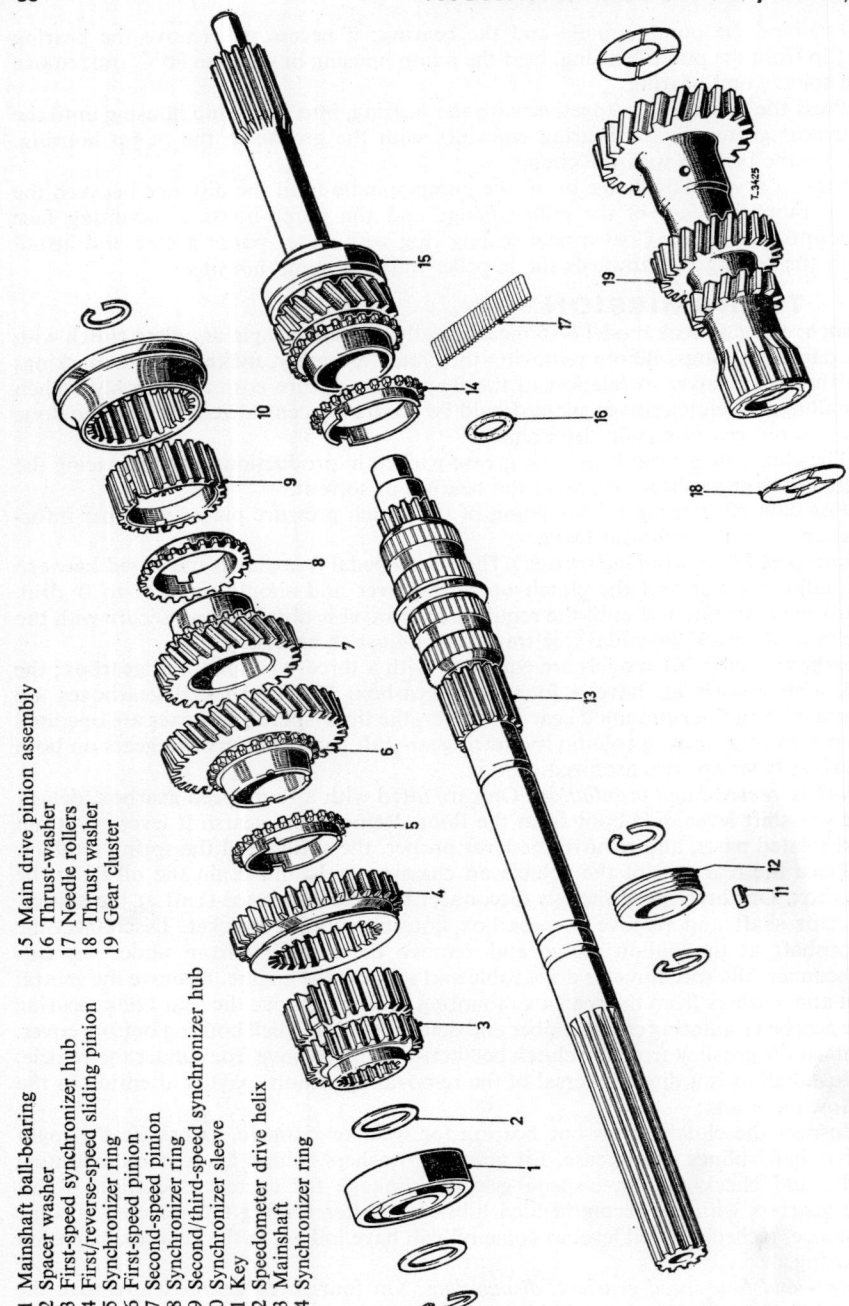

Fig. 24. Three-speed gearbox, gear trains

1 Mainshaft ball-bearing
2 Spacer washer
3 First-speed synchronizer hub
4 First/reverse-speed sliding pinion
5 Synchronizer ring
6 First-speed pinion
7 Second-speed pinion
8 Synchronizer ring
9 Second/third-speed synchronizer hub
10 Synchronizer sleeve
11 Key
12 Speedometer drive helix
13 Mainshaft
14 Synchronizer ring
15 Main drive pinion assembly
16 Thrust-washer
17 Needle rollers
18 Thrust washer
19 Gear cluster

the assembly in a vice. Remove the gearbox rear mounting, the speedometer drive housing and driven gear.

Remove the gearbox bottom cover.

On four-speed gearboxes, remove the reverse stop housing. Remove the bolts securing the gearbox extension housing to the gearbox and rotate the extension housing to expose the rear end of the secondary shaft.

With a suitable brass drift, tap out the secondary shaft towards the front, taking care not to lose the locking ball at its front end. Lift the gear cluster from the gearbox and discard the needle rollers and the thrust-washers.

Remove the selector finger locating screws, withdraw the selector and remove the selector fingers. Carefully remove the plugs from the gearbox casing and collect the shifter-fork shaft detent balls and springs. Drive out the shifter fork-to-shaft securing pins until the forks can slide freely on the shafts.

To drive out the securing pin of the first/reverse speed shifter fork, support the rear end of the shaft by engaging reverse gear.

Do not drive out the pins completely as they may jam on the gearbox casing.

With the aid of a brass drift, tap out the shifter-fork shafts toward the front; this will simultaneously drive out the end plugs. Take the shifter forks out of the gearbox. Extract the reverse pinion shaft and remove the pinion. Remove the five bolts securing the gearbox front cover and remove the main drive shaft, together with the bearing and cover.

Remove the gearbox mainshaft assembly, together with the gearbox extension housing.

If necessary, remove the selector-shaft oil-seal from its bore in the casing.

Remove the needle rollers from the spigot bearing recess in the rear end of the main drive shaft. Spread the main drive shaft ball-bearing retaining circlip and withdraw the pinion and bearing assembly from the cover by tapping the end of the shaft on a leaden or wooden block; remove the circlip from the shaft.

Remove the circlip from the gearbox front cover and fit it into the groove in the ball-bearing outer race.

Support the circlip on a suitable tube and press the main drive shaft out of the bearing; then remove the circlip from the bearing.

Remove the mainshaft rear bearing circlip from the gearbox extension housing and press the mainshaft assembly out of the housing.

NOTE: *The mainshaft rear bearing outer race is an interference fit in the aluminium extension housing bore; it may therefore be necessary to heat the cover to some extent before withdrawal of the bearing is possible.*

On four-speed gearboxes, mark the position of the first- and second-speed synchronizer hub, thereby ensuring correct assembly.

Remove the circlip retaining the speedometer drive helix; remove the helix and retain the key. Remove the remaining circlip from the mainshaft.

Remove the mainshaft rear bearing circlip and the thrust washer.

Mainshaft assembly, three-speed gearboxes: Support the assembly on the first-speed pinion front face and press out the mainshaft.

Slide the first-speed synchronizer sleeve and reverse speed pinion from the hub, and remove the detent springs and keys.

Next remove the exposed circlip and press the mainshaft out of the second/top-speed synchronizer hub by supporting the assembly on the second-speed pinion.

Slide the second/top-speed synchronizer sleeve from the hub and retain the detent springs and keys.

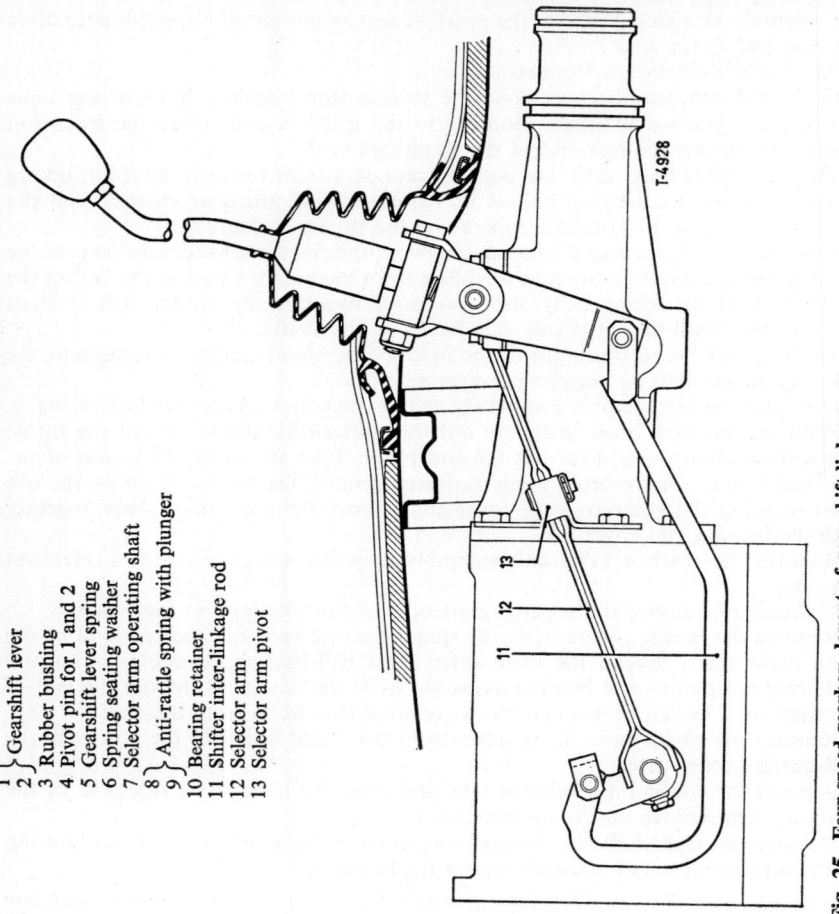

1 Gearshift lever
2 Rubber bushing
3 Pivot pin for 1 and 2
4 Gearshift lever spring
5 Spring seating washer
6 Selector arm operating shaft
7 Anti-rattle spring with plunger
8
9 Bearing retainer
10 Shifter inter-linkage rod
11 Selector arm
12 Selector arm pivot
13

Fig. 25. Four-speed gearbox, layout of gear-shift linkage

T-4928

Mainshaft assembly, four-speed gearboxes: Remove the third/top-speed synchron-izer hub retaining circlip from the front end of the mainshaft; support the rear face of the third-speed pinion and press out the mainshaft. Slide the synchronizer sleeve from its hub and retain the detent springs and keys.

Support the front face of the second-speed pinion and press out the mainshaft. Remove the synchronizer sleeve from its hub and retain the detent springs and keys.

Gearbox bottom cover, four-speed gearboxes: Remove the plug and collect the reverse-speed shifter-shaft detent ball and spring. Remove the shifter-shaft bore end-plugs. Position the shaft in such a manner that the striker fork to shaft securing pin lines up with the oil drain plug bore; then drive out the pin. Now move the shaft so that the striker fork retaining pin lines up with the drain plug hole; remove the striker fork retaining pin. Slide the shaft through the bore until the shifter-fork retaining pin lines-up with the drain plug hole; drive out the pin and slide out the shaft. Remove the striker fork and the shifter fork.

Carefully clean and examine the condition of all parts, replacing any parts that are worn or have otherwise become unserviceable.

The synchronizer hubs are to be serviced as an assembly, and no components of them should be replaced individually. If one or more pinions on the mainshaft need replacement, it is imperative to replace the gear cluster assembly as well, as otherwise silent operation of the gearbox cannot be guaranteed. The same applies if one of the gear cluster pinions is damaged, in which case the gear cluster as well as all mainshaft pinions must be renewed.

Carefully scrutinize the friction surface of each synchronizer ring for service-ability; renew as necessary.

Gearbox assembly:

Synchronizer units: The first-speed synchronizer unit on the three-speed gearboxes is assembled as follows:

Install the first synchronizer spring with both turned-out ends located in the groove in the hub.

Install the three sliding keys and position the spring in such a manner that one end is located in the slotted key. The detent pips on the sliding keys are centrally disposed, which allows their installation either way round.

Install the second spring so that its turned-out end engages in the slotted key.

The sliding keys and synchronizer springs of the second/top-speed synchronizer hub on the three-speed gearboxes, as well as of both synchronizer hubs on four-speed gearboxes, are fitted as follows:

Fit the sliding keys in such a manner that the pips on the keys are offset towards the spigoted end of the hub.

Install the synchronizer springs so that the turned-out extremity of each spring is located in the slotted key and the relative location of the springs is in accordance with the diagram shown in Fig. 28.

Assembling the mainshaft:

On three-speed gearboxes:

a   Fit the first-speed synchronizer ring on to its synchronizer hub, ensuring that the slots in the ring coincide with the synchronizer sliding keys.

b   Fit the first-speed pinion on to the synchronizer unit so that the cone of the pinion engages the first-speed synchronizer ring, and guide the rear end of the mainshaft through the assembly.

c   Rotate the mainshaft so that the splines coincide with those of the synchronizer hub and press the assembly home on the mainshaft. For this operation the use

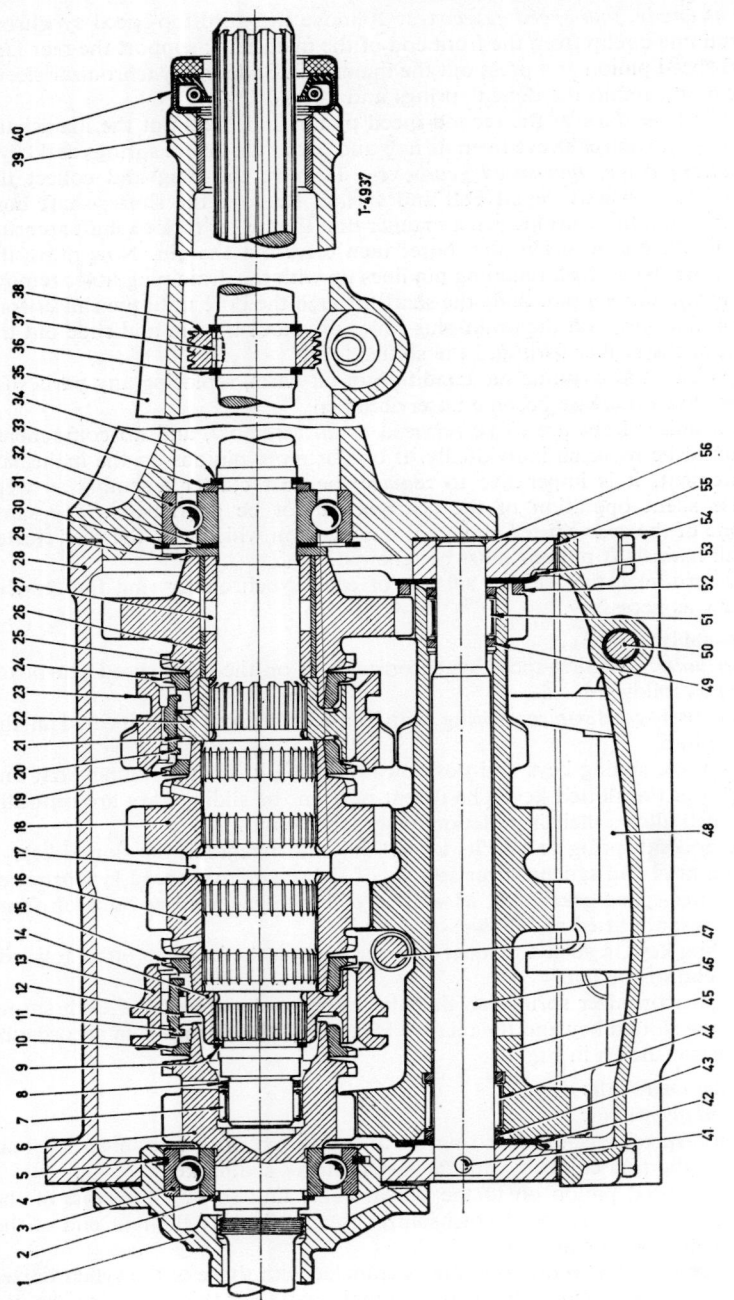

T-4937

Fig. 26. Four-speed gearbox, longitudinal section

Fig. 27. Four-speed gearbox and rear engine mounting (arrow indicates oil filler/level plug)

Key to Fig. 26:

1 Main drive pinion bearing cover	29 Thrust washer
2 Circlip	30 Circlip
3 Ball-bearing	31 Shim
4 Gasket	32 Ball-bearing
5 Circlip	33 Spacer washer
6 Main drive pinion	34 Circlip
7 Needle roller bearing	35 Gearbox extension housing
8 Thrust-washer for 7	36 Circlip
9 Circlip	37 Key for 38
10 Top-speed synchronizer ring	38 Speedometer drive helix
11 Synchronizer key	39 Bush
12 Synchronizer spring	40 Oil-seal
13 Third/top-speed synchronizer sleeve	41 Locking ball for 46
14 Third/top-speed synchronizer hub	42 Thrust washer
15 Third-speed synchronizer ring	43 Spacer-washer
16 Third-speed pinion	44 Gear cluster needle roller bearing
17 Mainshaft	45 Gear cluster
18 Second-speed pinion	46 Secondary shaft
19 Second-speed synchronizer ring	47 Shifter/selector shaft
20 Synchronizer key	48 Reverse-speed shifter-fork shaft
21 Synchronizer spring	49 Spacer washer
22 First/second-speed synchronizer hub	50 Detent assembly for 48
23 First/second-speed synchronizer sleeve	51 Gear cluster needle roller bearing
24 Synchronizer ring	52 Thrust-washer (non-replaceable)
25 First-speed pinion	53 Thrust-washer
26 Bush in pinion	54 Gearbox bottom cover
27 Spacer bush	55 Gasket
28 Gearbox housing	56 Gasket

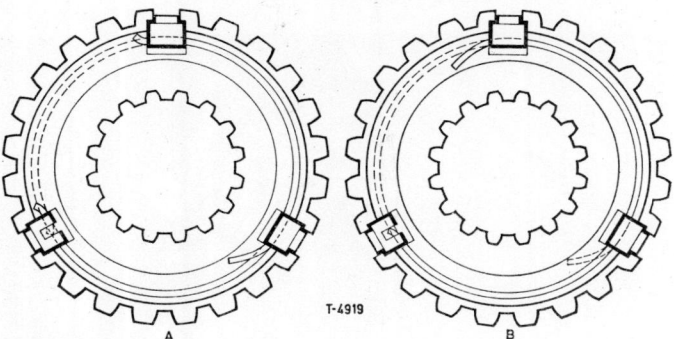

T-4919

A   First-speed synchronizer hub
B   Second/third-speed synchronizer hub (3-speed gearbox); first/second and third/top-speed synchronizer hub (4-speed gearbox)

Fig. 28. Positions of sliding key springs

of suitable press-bed adaptors is desirable. Prevent the components from tilting and so becoming seized on the shaft.

On four-speed gearboxes:

a   Fit the second-speed pinion onto the rear end of the mainshaft; then install the appropriate synchronizer ring. With the spigoted end towards the rear, fit the first/second-speed synchronizer hub onto the shaft.

b   Engage the slots of the synchronizer ring with the sliding keys in the synchronizer hub; align the splines on the mainshaft with the internal splines of the hub and press the assembly home onto the shaft, preferably with the aid of suitable press-bed adaptors.

c   Slide the first-speed pinion bush onto the rear end of the mainshaft and press fully home.

d   Slide the first/second-speed synchronizer sleeve onto the appropriate hub so that its shifter-fork groove is towards the rear end of the mainshaft.

e   Install the first-speed synchronizer ring, engaging its slots with the sliding keys in the synchronizer hub; then install the first-speed sliding pinion onto the bush and fit the thrust-washer with the chamfered face towards the rear of the mainshaft.

The mainshaft longitudinal location is determined by the mainshaft ball-bearing: it is therefore important that the bearing is in its proper location on the shaft. To obtain this, shims are interposed between the first/reverse-speed synchronizer hub rear abutment face and the ball-bearing on three-speed gearboxes, and between the mainshaft spacer-washer and the bearing on four-speed gearboxes.

The thickness of the shimpack required can be determined by a special gauge, which can be used on three-speed as well as on four-speed gearboxes.

Compose a shimpack of the required thickness and install on the shaft.

On three-speed gearboxes, install the first-speed synchronizer sleeve and reverse speed sliding pinion to the synchronizer hub, its shifter-fork groove towards the rear end of the mainshaft.

Slide a new bearing circlip onto the rear end of the mainshaft, followed by the bearing; then press the bearing fully home against the shims (where fitted), taking care that the shims and the circlip remain clear of the circlip groove in the mainshaft.

Install the mainshaft bearing thrust washer and select a circlip which will take up all clearance between the thrust-washer and the rear face of the circlip groove; install the circlip. These circlips are available in seven thicknesses.

Install the front speedometer drive helix circlip, followed by the helix proper, the chamfered face of which should be towards the front end of the mainshaft. Select one circlip which takes up all clearance between the rear face of the helix and the rear face of the circlip groove.

On three-speed gearboxes install the second-speed pinion, on four-speed gearboxes the third-speed; then fit the appropriate synchronizer ring.

Place the top-speed synchronizer hub with the spigoted end towards the front, onto the front end of the shaft. Engage the slots of the synchronizer ring with the sliding keys in the hub; engage the internal splines of the hub with the splines on the shaft and press home the hub.

Select a new circlip which will take up all clearance between the synchronizer hub spigot and the front face of the circlip groove.

Slide the top-speed synchronizer sleeve onto the hub so that the shifter-fork groove is towards the front end of the mainshaft.

Insert a spare propeller-shaft sliding yoke into the extension-housing bush; this is to avoid damaging the bush when installing the mainshaft.

Carefully guide the mainshaft splined rear end into the gearbox extension housing and engage with the splines in the dummy sleeve.

Locate the mainshaft ball-bearing in the housing and press fully home.

NOTE: *The mainshaft ball-bearing is an interference fit in the gearbox extension housing; it may therefore be necessary to warm the housing to some extent before the bearing can be pressed in.*

Install the bearing retaining circlip, ensuring that it is properly located in the groove.

Install the needle bearing spacer on the spigot at the front end of the mainshaft and retain with a smear of stiff grease.

Main drive shaft and bearing assembly: Press the ball-bearing onto the main drive shaft so that the bearing circlip groove is nearest to the main drive pinion. Install a new circlip to retain the ball-bearing on the shaft.

Fit a new circlip in the groove in the main drive shaft bearing bore and insert the main drive shaft assembly into the cover.

Lightly clamp the main drive shaft bearing cover in a vice, the jaws of which must be protected with wooden blocks; expand the bearing circlip in the cover and tap the main drive shaft and bearing assembly home into the cover with a rubber-faced mallet. Ensure that the circlip fully engages with the groove in the bearing outer race.

Smear some petroleum jelly in the main drive shaft counter bore and install the 24 needle rollers. Do not apply more grease than is necessary to retain the needle rollers, as otherwise the oil passages will become clogged.

Place a needle roller spacer into the gear cluster rear counter bore; apply a smear of petroleum jelly and install 25 needle rollers, followed by the other spacer.

NOTE: *The spacers used for the rear counter bore are smaller in diameter than those used in the front counter bore.*

Fit the larger spacers and 26 needle rollers to the front counter bore. Smear the front jointing face of the extension housing with grease and install a new gasket.

Carefully insert the mainshaft into the gearbox casing and swivel the extension housing round the mainshaft so that the reverse-speed pinion shaft bore is accessible for installation of the reverse-speed pinion shaft.

Hold the reverse-speed pinion with the chamfered end towards the front in position in the gearbox; install the reverse-speed pinion shaft using a brass drift. Ensure that the ball in the end of the shaft corresponds with the recess in the gearbox housing.

Rotate the gearbox extension housing back into the correct position.

On early four-speed gearboxes secure the selector/shifter-shaft fulcrum bracket with the two longer bolts and install the remaining bolts, without tightening them. If this precaution is disregarded, a pneumatic lock may be created when the countershaft is driven home.

Sparingly apply a coat of sealing compound to the main drive shaft bearing cover rear face and stick a new gasket to the bearing cover.

Install the top-speed synchronizer ring and carefully insert the main drive shaft assembly, engaging the mainshaft spigot with the main drive gear counter bore. Make sure that the slots of the top-speed synchronizer ring engage with the keys of the relative synchronizer hub.

Install and tighten the main drive shaft bearing cover bolts, using new copper washers.

Hold the shifter forks in position and insert the shifter-fork shafts from the front end of the casing.

NOTE: *The prongs on the top-speed shifter forks are of equal length.*

On four-speed gearboxes install the first- and second-speed shifter fork on the shifter-fork shaft, so that the jaw of the fork is facing towards the front of the gearbox and is in alignment with the machined position of the shaft.

Secure each shifter fork with a new pin. On four-speed gearboxes the shorter pin is used for the first/second-speed shifter fork.

NOTE: *On three-speed gearboxes, reverse gear should be selected in order to support the rear of the shifter-fork shaft when securing the first/reverse gear shifter fork.*

When correctly installed, the shifter-fork securing pins are in the vertical plane.

Install the shifter-fork shaft bore end-plugs (open end leading) in the front of the housing and drive them home until they are flush with the gearbox front face.

With the aid of a suitable drift, fit a new selector/shifter shaft oil-seal, ensuring that its lip is turned towards the inside of the gearbox housing.

Insert the selector shifter shaft into the lubricated oil-seal so as to pick up the selector levers on its way through.

On four-speed gearboxes the longer prong of the third/top-speed selector lever must be turned towards the bottom of the gearbox housing.

Tighten the selector lever locating screws to the specified torque (see Technical Data).

On four-speed gearboxes, install a new oil-seal in the shifter/selector-shaft counter bore in the casing; then fit the reverse stop housing. Install the reverse speed detent ball and spring, fit the fibre washer and the special screw.

With a smear of grease stick the gear cluster thrust-washers into position on the thrust faces of the gear. The front thrust-washer has a flat on its circumference for identification purposes; do not interchange the thrust-washers.

Hold the gear cluster in position in the gearbox and ensure that the thrust-washers are properly located; then insert the countershaft and align the locating ball on its front end with the recess in the gearbox front face. Fully tighten the gearbox extension housing securing bolts.

On four-speed gearboxes, install the reverse-speed selector/shifter-fork shaft, shifter shaft and selector as follows:

Insert the selector/shifter-fork shaft into the bottom cover with the detent ball grooves towards the rear so as to pick up the selector and the shifter fork on its way through. The selector must be positioned so that its retaining pin hole offset is towards the centre of the cover.

Secure the selector and the shifter fork with new retaining pins and drive the pins in until they are flush with the fork boss.

Install a new end plug in each end of the shaft bore.

Insert the selector/shifter-fork shaft detent ball and spring, and fully tighten the securing plug.

Install the bottom cover, ensuring that the reverse-speed shifter fork properly engages the groove in the reverse -speed pinion.

Place the gearbox upside down in the vice and insert the shifter-fork shaft detent balls and springs; fit the fibre washers, followed by the detent spring locating screws.

Fit a new oil-seal into the speedometer drive gear housing; fit the speedometer driven gear and install the housing in the position as shown in the figures below.

On four-speed gearboxes, refit the gearshift linkage and check for proper functioning of the gearshift mechanism. Before installation in the vehicle, remove the gearshift lever.

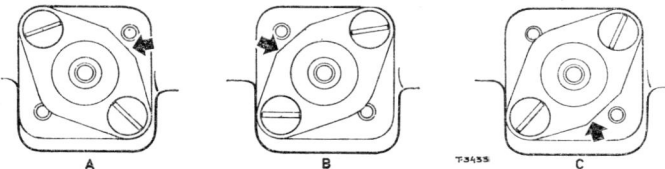

Fig. 29. Speedometer drive location

Rear axle ratio	Tyre size	Number of teeth on speedometer driven gear	Location of flat on speedometer drive housing
3·9 : 1 (10/39)	5.60–13	17	A
	5.90–13	16	B
4·125 : 1 (8/33)	5.60–13	18	A
	5.90–13	17	A
4·625 : 1 (8/37)	5.60–13	20	C
	5.90–13	19	C

Powerglide automatic transmission: This transmission, which is an optional extra on all FC models, consists of a hydraulically-operated compound planetary gear train providing two forward ratios and reverse, coupled to a three-element torque converter.

In view of the specialized knowledge and tools which are required, no instructions are given here for adjustments, repairs and overhauls. This should be left to authorised specialists. For general data and regular maintenace instructions, refer to pages 15 and 19.

A longitudinal section of the Powerglide, showing the main components, is shown in Fig. 30.

Propeller shaft: The Vauxhall Victor 101 and VX 4/90 are equipped with either a Hardy Spicer or BRD propeller shaft; these can be identified by the name Hardy or BRD cast on the propeller-shaft yoke. When servicing or overhauling universal joints, ensure that replacement parts are of the correct make. The rearmost universal joint is fitted with a coupling flange, which is bolted onto the final-drive pinion

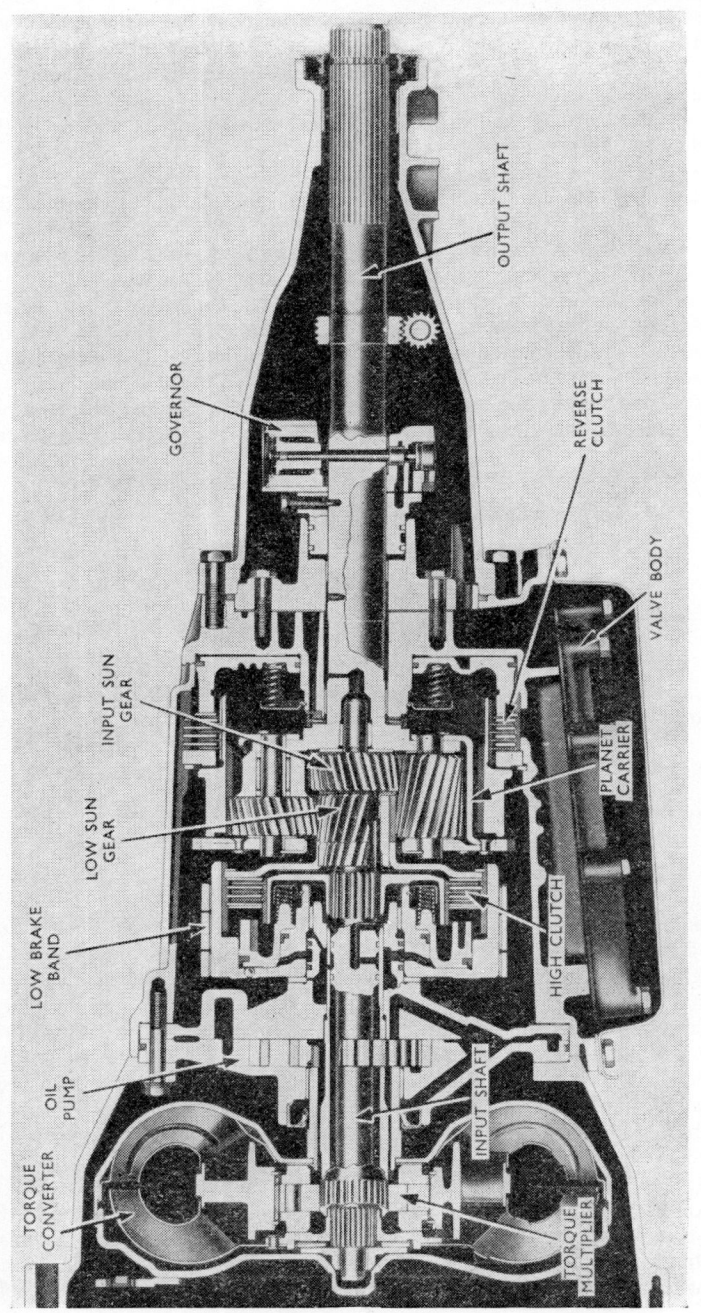

Fig. 30. Powerglide automatic transmission, longitudinal section

flange; the front universal joint has internal splines which correspond to the splines on the gearbox mainshaft, thereby providing a sliding joint which compensates for the movement of the rear axle.

The universal joint needle rollers are grease-packed in production and do not require periodical lubrication.

If the universal joints are worn, overhaul is carried out in the usual manner. When withdrawing the propeller-shaft sliding yoke from the gearbox, it is imperative that a dummy sliding yoke be inserted to prevent oil flowing out of the gearbox. The propeller-shaft coupling bolts should be fitted with the bolt heads towards the U-joint.

Rear axle/Differential: Semi-floating rear axle with hypoid pinion and crownwheel. The pinion depth adjustment shims are situated behind the pinion rear bearing race in the differential housing. The pinion bearing pre-load is obtained by means of a collapsible spacing bush, which should always be renewed when repairs are carried out on the pinion and/or pinion bearings. The differential end-float, as well as the necessary backlash of the crownwheel teeth in relation to the pinion, is adjusted by means of shims which are interposed between the differential bearing outer races and the differential casing.

The differential bearings are retained by means of bearing caps, secured to the differential housing.

FCW and FCG (Estate Car) models are equipped with heavier rear wheel bearings with separate oil-seals.

Removal and installation: Place the rear of the car on chassis stands and remove the rear road wheels.

Disconnect the propeller shaft rear coupling flange and detach the parking brake front cable from the equalizer lever on the rear axle housing.

Disconnect the hydraulic brake pipe at the wheel cylinders. Remove one of the parking brake rear cable pivot pins and detach the parking brake cable from the slot in the pivot pin; withdraw the cable. Remove the spring anchor plate nuts and remove each plate from the bolts.

Raise the assembly clear of the springs and remove it from underneath the vehicle.

Installation is a reversal of the above operation.

The spring insulators should not be interchanged; worn spring seats should be renewed. Top-up the oil level in the differential housing with the recommended lubricant and bleed the brake system.

Dismantling the rear axle/differential units: Rest the assembly on an axle stand, drain the oil and remove the rear cover plate, together with its gasket. Remove both half-shafts as detailed on page 51; on FCG and FCW (Estate Car) models, also remove the oil-seals.

Remove the differential bearing caps after having marked the right-hand side bearing cap in relation to the housing with, for example, the letter 'X.' With the aid of a long, flat bar, lever the differential assembly out of the housing by placing the extremity of the bar under one of the crownwheel attaching bolts. Remove the thrust washers, the adjustment shims and the differential bearing outer races, taking care not to interchange these.

Remove the final drive pinion flange retaining nut and withdraw the flange and the oil-seal.

Gently tap the pinion out of the housing. Remove the collapsible bearing spacer and the thrust washer from the housing if they were not released together with the pinion. Press the pinion rear and front bearing outer races out of the axle housing

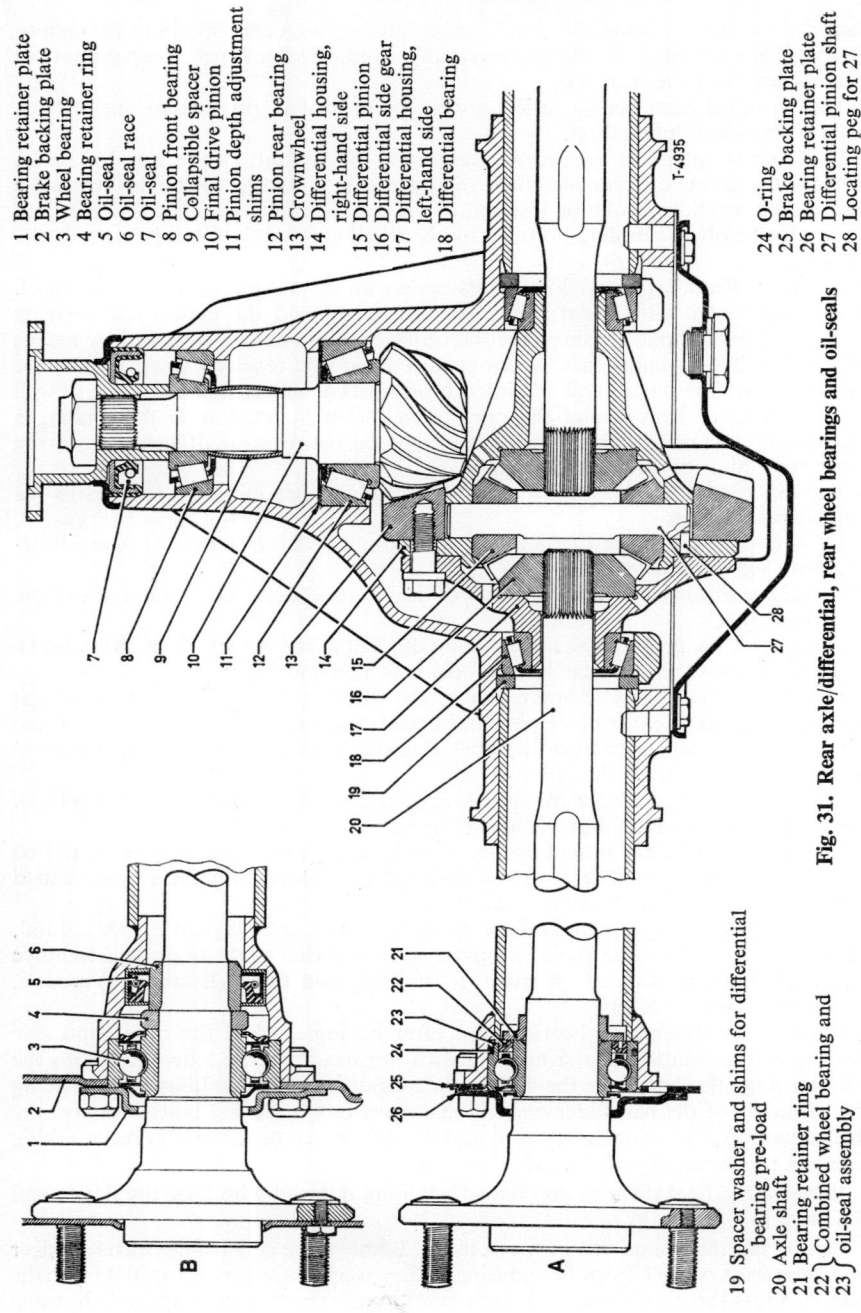

1 Bearing retainer plate
2 Brake backing plate
3 Wheel bearing
4 Bearing retainer ring
5 Oil-seal
6 Oil-seal race
7 Oil-seal
8 Pinion front bearing
9 Collapsible spacer
10 Final drive pinion
11 Pinion depth adjustment
    shims
12 Pinion rear bearing
13 Crownwheel
14 Differential housing,
    right-hand side
15 Differential pinion
16 Differential side gear
17 Differential housing,
    left-hand side
18 Differential bearing

19 Spacer washer and shims for differential
    bearing pre-load
20 Axle shaft
21 Bearing retainer ring
22 Combined wheel bearing and
23 oil-seal assembly

24 O-ring
25 Brake backing plate
26 Bearing retainer plate
27 Differential pinion shaft
28 Locating peg for 27

T-4935

Fig. 31. Rear axle/differential, rear wheel bearings and oil-seals

and make a note of the number and thickness of the shim(s) used for the pinion depth adjustment. If the pinion has 10 teeth, special tool Z8519 is required to remove the pinion rear bearing. Remove the crownwheel attaching bolts and carefully tap the crownwheel from its seating.

Separate both differential carrier halves and remove the free differential side gear from the housing half.

Remove the differential pinion shaft, collect the differential pinions and finally remove the remaining differential side gear.

Thoroughly clean and inspect all parts, renewing all parts needing replacement.

Removal of a half-shaft and rear wheel bearing: Place the rear end of the car on suitable chassis stands and remove the road wheel; release the parking brake and remove the rear brake drum. Remove the wheel bearing retainer plate securing nuts and withdraw the half-shaft, complete with bearing assembly, from the rear axle tube. If necessary, remove the wheel bearing from the half-shaft by splitting the bearing retaining ring with a chisel (this also applies to the oil-seal boss on FCW and FCG models). Support the bearing and press out the half-shaft. Except on FCW and FCG models, the oil-seal is incorporated in the rear wheel bearing; in case of a defective oil-seal, it is necessary to replace the bearing as well. Thoroughly inspect the half-shaft for distortion or worn splines and replace if necessary.

Slightly marked sealing faces of seal bosses on FCG and FCW models can be restored with very fine sandpaper.

Installation of a half-shaft and rear wheel bearing: All models, except FCG and FCW, proceed as follows:

Press a new rear wheel bearing, with its oil-seal facing the differential, onto the half-shaft, then with the aid of a suitable tool (for example, a length of tube) press on a new bearing retaining ring with its collar towards the bearing. Install a new sealing ring coated with oil into the groove on the bearing outer race and place a new gasket onto the bearing retaining plate; ensure that the hole in the gasket corresponds with the hole in the brake backing plate.

On FCG and FCW models proceed as follows: If necessary, press a new oil-seal, lubricated with oil, into the groove; the oil-seal periphery should be 1·2in away from the brake backing plate mounting flange. Press a new ball-bearing onto the half-shaft, heat a new bearing retaining ring until it assumes a blue colour, then press it onto the shaft with the chamfered side turned away from the bearing; the pressing-on can be accomplished with the aid of service tool SE.525. Keep applying pressure to the retaining ring until it is completely cooled down. Press the oil-seal boss onto the shaft and against the bearing retaining ring; its chamfered outer periphery should be turned away from the bearing.

When inserting the half-shaft assembly, take care not to damage the oil-seal; for this purpose a half-shaft guide is available.

Further installation is a reversal of the removal operation.

After completion, do not forget to check the oil level in the differential housing.

Assembling the rear axle/differential unit: Assemble the differential carrier, the differential pinions, the differential pinion shaft and the differential side gears with the thrust-washers, having first dipped all parts in the recommended lubricant. Join both differential carrier halves, taking care that the dowel engages the corresponding hole in the other half. Heat the crownwheel on a hot plate and screw two guide bolts diagonally into the crownwheel attaching bolt holes. Quickly install the crownwheel and secure with the attaching bolts and new lock-washers; tighten the bolts to a torque of 35–40ft lb. Determine the thickness of the differential

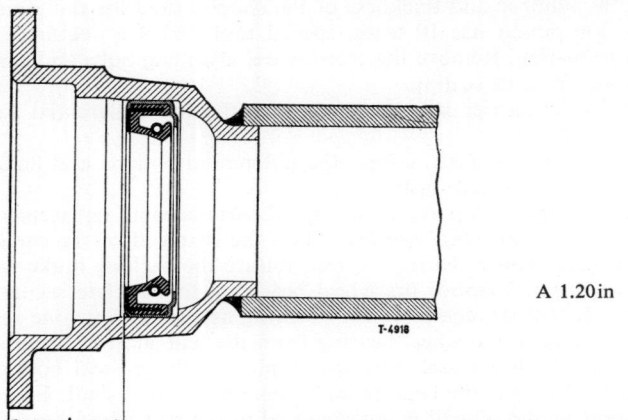

A 1.20 in

Fig. 32. Rear axle, FCW and FCG models, location of oil-seal

bearing pre-load adjustment shims as follows: Press both differential bearings onto the differential carrier, ensuring that the bearing inner races are pressed fully home. Install this assembly into the differential casing. Select four spacers and the required number of shims to eliminate all end-float between the differential bearing races and the inner ends of the axle housing tubes; remove differential from the casing.

Install two of the selected spacers with half of the shims interposed between them in one side of the housing and interpose the remaining shims plus one more between the other two spacers; insert this pack in the other side of the housing.

Locate the differential assembly in the housing, taking care that the differential bearing outer races do not tilt and jam.

Install the differential bearing caps in their original positions as indicated by the 'X' marking on the right-hand side bearing cap. Install and tighten the bolts to the specified torque. Wind a length of twine round the differential and with a spring balance attached to the end of it, check the force required to rotate the assembly.

If necessary, the pre-load can be altered by adding or removing shims or changing the spacer thickness until the specified pre-load is obtained.

With the differential unit installed, mount a dial indicator on the casing and allow its stylus to rest perpendicularly against the back of the crownwheel. Rotate the differential and check the lateral run-out; this should not exceed the specified maximum.

Excessive run-out may be caused by improperly cleaned differential carrier mating faces. When a satisfactory reading has been obtained, remove the dial indicator and the differential unit, keeping the selected spacers and shims in each place so that they can be refitted in their original positions.

Determining the thickness of the pinion rear bearing shim: Check whether the pinion rear bearing is perfectly clean and install it on the special measuring jig. Tighten the knurled nut of the tool sufficiently to compress the Thackeray washer.

Allow the bearing to settle by rotating its outer race backwards and forwards through a few degrees.

With the aid of a micrometer, measure the overall dimension of the bearing and jig plate at two different points. From the obtained value, subtract the thickness of the jig plate; this dimension is etched-in in the plate. The value thus obtained represents the overall dimension of the pinion bearing.

The lateral position of the pinion in relation to the crownwheel is obtained by shims fitted between the pinion rear bearing outer race and the bearing abutment face in the housing. Shims are available in thicknesses of 0·003, 0·005 and 0·010 in. Increasing the number of shims results in moving the pinion towards the crownwheel, whereas reducing the number of shims moves the pinion away from the crownwheel. Shimming compensates for the machining tolerances of the pinion, the crownwheel and relative parts. The three factors which determine the total thickness of the pinion adjustment shims are as follows:

1. *The pinion rear bearing overall dimension:*
   The thickness of the corrective shim is determined by subtracting the actual bearing dimension from the maximum dimension of 0·9626 in.

2. *The depth of the pinion rear bearing abutment face:*
   Thickness of the shims required to justify any deviation from the nominal abutment face depth is marked on the axle casing cover plate mounting face. The stamped-in figure represents the shim thickness in thousands of an inch.

3. *Deviation from nominal pinion depth:*
   The pinion and crownwheel are a matched pair, machined to very close limits; machining tolerances, however, do occur; these tolerances are known to the manufacturer and the thickness of the necessary corrective shims to compensate for the tolerance of a particular pinion set is marked in thousandths of an inch on the pinion nose.

To obtain the correct shim thickness, add the following:

1. The pinion bearing correction.
2. The axle casing correction (indicated on housing).
3. The pinion depth correction (indicated on pinion nose).

The total value represents the total thickness of the pinion depth adjustment shim.

Example of calculation:

Pinion rear bearing, maximum dimension:	0·9626 in
Subtract:	
Actual dimension of pinion rear bearing:	0·9565 in
	———
Difference equals shim correction for bearing:	0·0061 in
To this value add:	
Axle casing correction (item 1), e.g. 2:	0·0020 in
Pinion depth correction (marked on pinion head), e.g. 5:	0·0050 in
	———
Total thickness of shims required is:	0·0131 in

The result should be rounded-off to the nearest thousandth of an inch; therefore, in case of the above example, the total thickness of the corrective shims amounts to 0·013 in.

Installation of the pinion: Press the pinion rear bearing inner race onto the pinion until it seats tightly against the pinion shoulder.

Place the original shimpack or that composed as described above on the rear bearing abutment face and press home the pinion rear bearing outer race; this can be accomplished with the aid of special drifts.

Press the pinion front bearing outer race into the housing.

Position the front bearing inner race and roller assembly in the housing, followed by a new oil-seal with the lip of the seal towards the pinion head. Tap the seal home with a suitable drift.

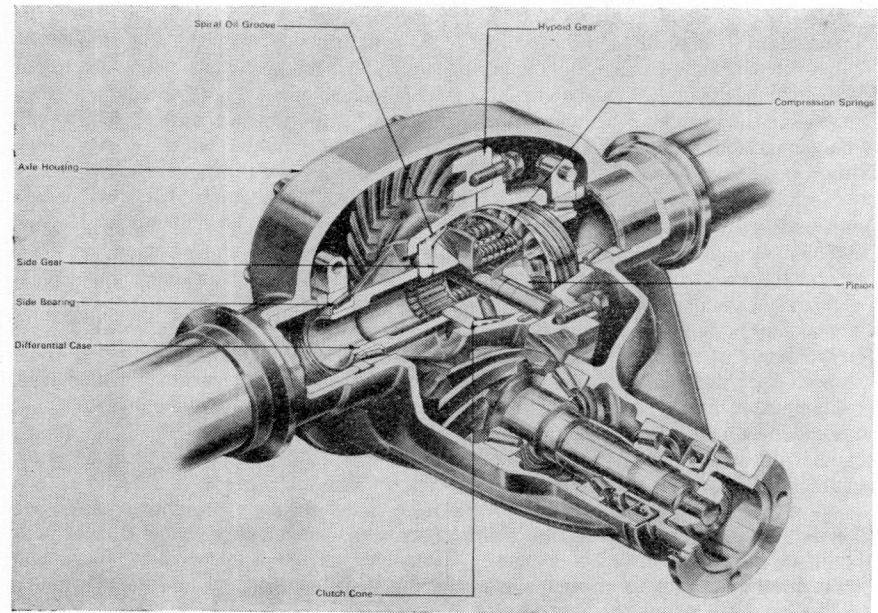

Fig. 33. Super Traction limited slip differential, partly cut-away view

Install a new collapsible spacer on the pinion shaft and insert the assembly into the housing until the pinion front end protrudes from the front bearing inner race. Lubricate the oil-seal boss of the companion flange with oil and slide the flange onto the pinion splines as far as it will go, or at least sufficiently to install the pinion nut.

Using a suitable pinion holding tool, tighten the pinion nut until a definite resistance is encountered; this indicates that all end-float between the bearing inner races and the collapsible spacer is eliminated. At this stage, there will still be a certain end-float between the bearing rollers and the outer races. Tighten the nut further whilst constantly checking with a pre-load gauge or torque meter, until the requisite bearing end-float of 8 to 11 lb in for new bearings, or 4 lb in for used bearings, is obtained. Do not exceed the requisite pre-load limit by overtightening the pinion nut, as this will necessitate replacement of the collapsible spacer.

Do not lock the pinion nut at this stage.

NOTE: *As from chassis serial number FC-6225110 (late 1966), a new pre-shaped pinion bearing pre-load spacer was introduced, in order to enable the initial fitting to be obtained more easily and to ensure that the spacer collapses correctly. The new spacer is not interchangeable with the old, because the spacer locating shoulder on the pinion shaft has been repositioned to accommodate the new spacer. New hypoid gear and pinion sets will service the old provided the revised spacers are used.*

Fit the oil filter pad and retainer into the axle casing.

Install the differential bearing spacers and the shims, ensuring that the greater number of shims is interposed between the spacers at the right-hand side of the casing.

Install the differential unit, mount a dial indicator on the casing and check the drive pinion to crownwheel teeth backlash.

If necessary, transfer one or more adjustment shims from one side of the differential to the other until the requisite amount of backlash is obtained. For specifications and tolerances refer to Technical Data.

NOTE: *Never change the total spacer and shim thickness in an attempt to adjust the backlash, as this will affect the differential bearing pre-load.*

Install the differential bearing caps and tighten the nuts to a torque of 22 to 25 ft lb.

It is recommended that the pinion-to-crownwheel tooth contact be checked in the conventional manner, using mechanic's blue.

Further assembly is a reversal of the dismantling procedure.

Super Traction differential:

The Super Traction limited slip-type differential serves to divert the drive from a wheel which is spinning on a muddy or otherwise slippery road surface to the wheel which has a better grip on the road; if, however, adhesion is so poor that a predetermined torque value cannot be attained, the slipping cones will disengage, which is noticeable by a continuous light whining sound.

The Super Traction differential also provides considerably improved cornering stability of the vehicle.

Dismantling and reassembly: The differential housing is identified by the letter 'L' adjacent to the rear axle ratio markings; there is also a label on the oil filler plug which draws attention to the fact that in this unit special hypoid oil is used.

When assembling the unit, be sure not to interchange the slipping cones so that they can be installed in their original positions. When shims are fitted between the cones and the differential side gears, do not forget to make a note of their thickness and location. Adjustment shims are available in thicknesses of $0 \cdot 005$ and $0 \cdot 010$ in.

Thoroughly clean and inspect all parts, replacing them as necessary.

The cone seats in the differential housing and the land surfaces on the heavy spirals of the cones should be smooth and should not show excessive scoring. Slight grooves and/or scratches are permissible and normal, and is no reason for replacement.

The amount of wear on the cones and differential housing is checked as follows:

Fit a cone to the relative differential housing half and, with a depth gauge, measure the distance between the inner side of the cone and the machined differential housing face; the maximum permissible distance at this point is $1 \cdot 114$ in, measured without shims. For the sake of clarity, call this dimension 'A' for later reference.

If this distance is greater than $1 \cdot 114$ in, the cone, as well as the pertaining differential housing half, should be renewed.

If the distance measured is within the permissible limit, install shims on the side of the cone to which the differential side gear is fitted. The correct shim thickness can be found in the table below (page 57).

Make sure that the differential side gears and the cones slide freely on the splines of the axle shafts.

The differential housing and cones should be serviced as an assembly; no parts thereof should be replaced individually.

Be sure that the adjustment shims (if fitted) are not transposed side for side.

NOTE: *When reassembling the differential unit, use the support plate SE.819 and adaptor SE.820 to ensure correct gear and cone spline alignment.*

Incorrect alignment of the differential side-gear splines and those in the cones

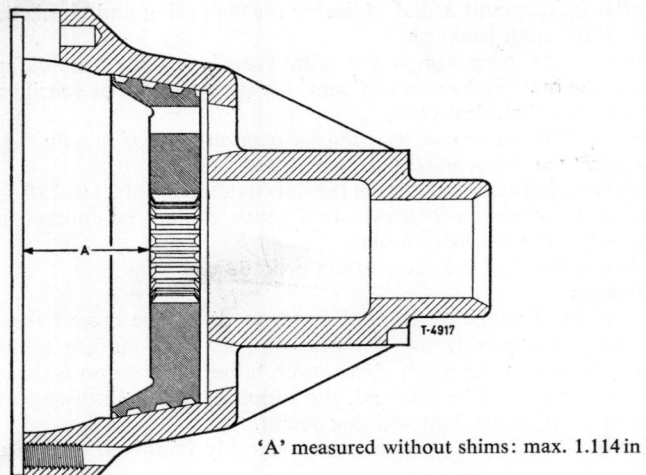

'A' measured without shims: max. 1.114 in

Fig. 34. Super Traction differential, case and cone installation

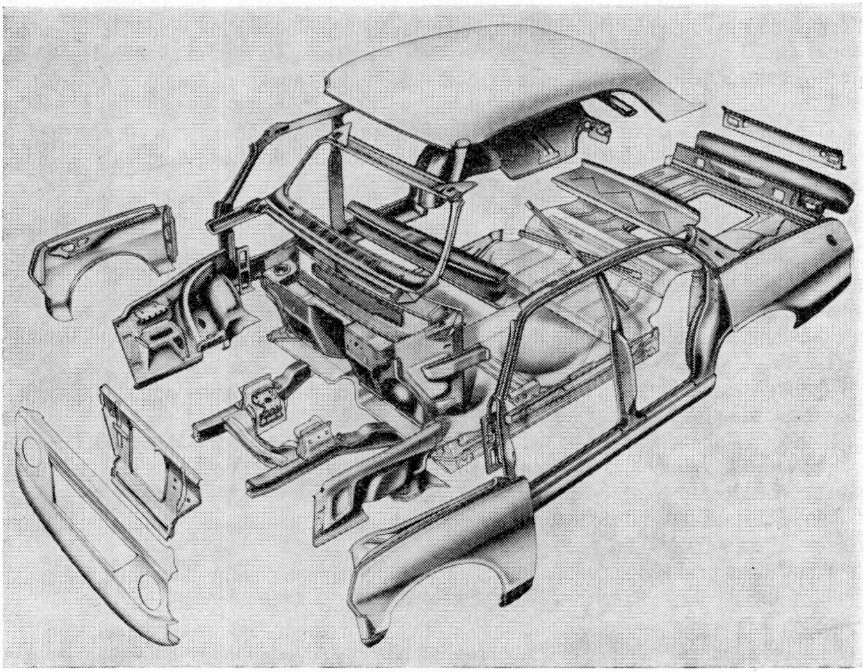

Fig. 35. Chassis/body shell structure, saloon, exploded view

will render installation of the axle shafts impossible upon final assembly.

Never use force when inserting the axle shafts or damage to the cone splines will result.

Before assembly, immerse all parts in clean lubricant of the recommended kind to provide adequate lubrication on initial operation; then assemble as follows:

Clamp the support plate in a vice.

Place the differential housing over the support with the interior of the casing uppermost. Install the appropriate cone on the spline of the support, followed by the correct thickness shim (if fitted); then install the differential side gear.

Place a thrust block on top of the gear, the cut-out in the block should coincide with the differential pinion shaft groove in the housing.

Install the differential pinion shaft, the pinion and the thrust-washers.

Insert the shaft so that the retaining pin hole lines-up with the hole in the housing, and insert the pin.

Install the thrust springs, followed by the second thrust block.

Install a shim (if fitted) on the differential side gear, and place the cone on the gear.

Place the differential housing cover over the cone; ensure that the markings stamped on both housing halves coincide.

Screw a bolt into two diagonally opposed holes and tighten by hand only. Insert the adaptor through the housing cover and turn to engage the splines of the cone and the side gear. Leaving the adaptor *in situ*, insert and tighten the remaining bolts to a torque of 12 ft lb.

With a torque wrench on the adaptor, check the operation of the unit; before slipping occurs, the torque reading should not be less than 75 ft lb.

For further assembly and installation proceed as outlined for the conventional differential unit.

Important. After installing the differential in the axle housing, do not attempt to rotate the assembly by the axle shaft if the second shaft is not fitted, as this will cause misalignment of the internal splines which prevents entry of the second shaft.

After installation in the vehicle, do not forget to fill the housing with the recommended type of special hypoid lubricant (see Lubrication and Maintenance, page 20).

Adjustment shim specifications:

Dimension 'A'	Shim thickness required
1·9040–1·0999 in	none
1·1000–1·1049 in	0·005 in
1·1050–1·1090 in	0·010 in
1·1090–1·1140 in	0·015 in

CHASSIS

Chassis: The chassis and the body are welded together to form a single unit. For chassis/body dimensions refer to Fig. 36.

Front wheel suspension: Independent front suspension by means of unequal length wishbones, coil springs, double-acting hydraulic shock-absorbers and an anti-roll bar. The suspension arms are attached to a cross-member which is incorporated in the front sub-frame; this sub-frame is available as a separate unit. The front suspension pivot shafts are mounted in Silentbloc bearings which do not require any maintenance.

Different coil springs giving alternative riding height and suspension characteristics are available.

Removal and installation of the front suspension (one side):

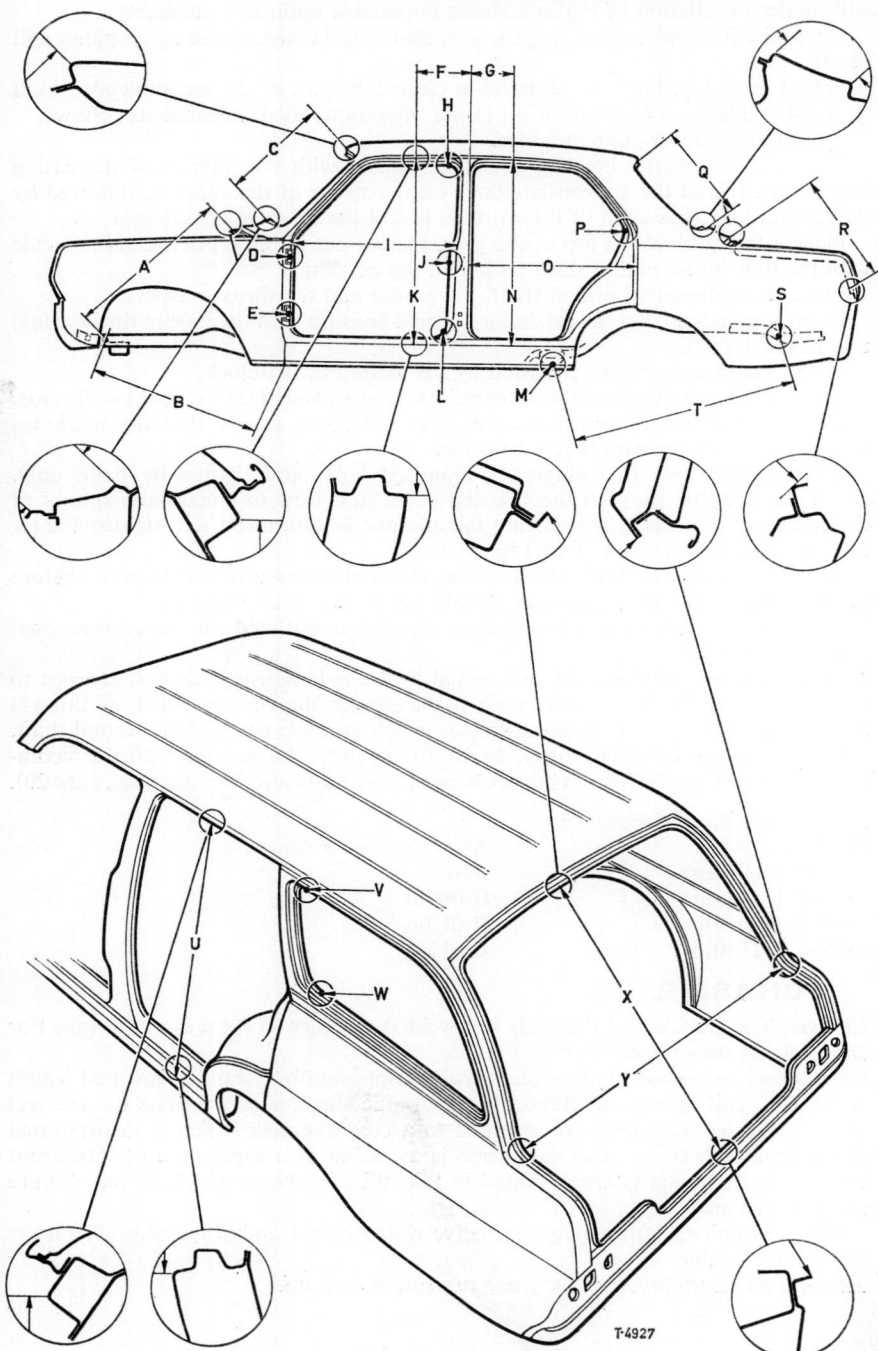

T-4927

Fig. 36. Chassis/body shell structure, saloon and estate car, dimensions and sections

Jack-up the front of the vehicle, support it on a chassis stand and remove the road wheel with hub/brake drum assembly. On VX 4/90 models remove the disc brake caliper and the hub/brake disc assembly; support the caliper assembly so that the hydraulic hose is not stressed.

Jack-up the outer end of the lower suspension arm, detach the anti-roll bar and the shock-absorber lower mounting plate; remove the shock-absorber.

Slacken off the lower ball-joint by one turn; tap the tapered nut part of the bolt out of the bore and remove the nut. Place a wooden block between the upper suspension arm and the chassis cross-member and with the aid of a suitable spring compressing tool, install hooks on as many coils as possible.

Lower the jack and remove the coil spring with the rubber pad.

With the aid of an extractor, detach the steering track rod knuckle from the wheel track-rod arm.

Detach the lower suspension arm from the cross-member and make a note of the number and location of the camber and caster adjustment shims to ensure correct replacement when installing.

Remove the brake backing plate (except on VX 4/90 models) and suspend it so that it is out of the way and the hydraulic hose is not stressed.

Loosen the upper ball-joint nut by one turn, tap the tapered portion of the bolt out of its bore and remove the nut. Remove the wheel swivel assembly from underneath the car.

Detach the upper suspension arm from the cross-member and make a note of the number and location of the camber and caster adjustment shims to ensure replacement in the correct position.

If necessary, remove the wheel swivel ball-joints from the suspension arms with the aid of tools SE 720 and 719.

The suspension arm bushes can be replaced in the conventional manner.

Installation is a reversal of the above operations but note the following points:

Ensure that the coil spring lower extremity is properly seated in the recess in the suspension arm and be sure to secure the shock-absorber lower mounting before removing the coil spring compressing tool.

When pressing-in new wheel swivel ball-joints, note the correct location of the grease nipples. Before tightening the lower suspension arm attaching nuts, bounce the car up and down a few times to settle the mountings; always use new locking plates.

New wheel swivel ball-joints should be lubricated with grease. Upon completion of installation check the front wheel alignment. For specifications refer to *Technical Data.*

Checking the riding height, front: Place the car on absolutely level ground and ensure that the front wheels are in the straight-ahead position.

Measurement should be carried out with car at kerb weight (i.e., unladen and with fuel tank full).

Key to Fig. 36:
Dimensions in inches

A   36.06 (measured at longitudinal centre-line of car)

B   42.50

C   22.80

D ⎫
E ⎬ 61.24 (measured at hinge pin centre-line, perpendicularly to longitudinal centre-line of car)

F	10.00	K	40.00	P	52.70	U	39.86
G	8.50	L	53.30	Q	19.90	V	46.76
H	43.68	M	42.24	R	27.05	W	56.00
I	34.77	N	39.90	S	37.12	X	40.36
J	53.30	O	35.80	T	47.40	Y	56.00

E

1 Front wheel inner bearing
2 Hub
3 Front wheel outer bearing
4 Castellated nut
5 Thrust-washer
6 Brake drum
7 Brake backing plate

8 Wheel-swivel assembly
9 Wheel swivel upper ball-joint
10 Upper bump rubber
11 Spring locating pad
12 Fulcrum shaft securing bolt
13 Engine mounting bracket
14 Cross-member
15 Wheel-swivel lower ball-joint
16 Wheel-swivel abutment
17 Anti-roll bar securing bolt
18 Anti-roll bar
19 Reinforcement cross-rod

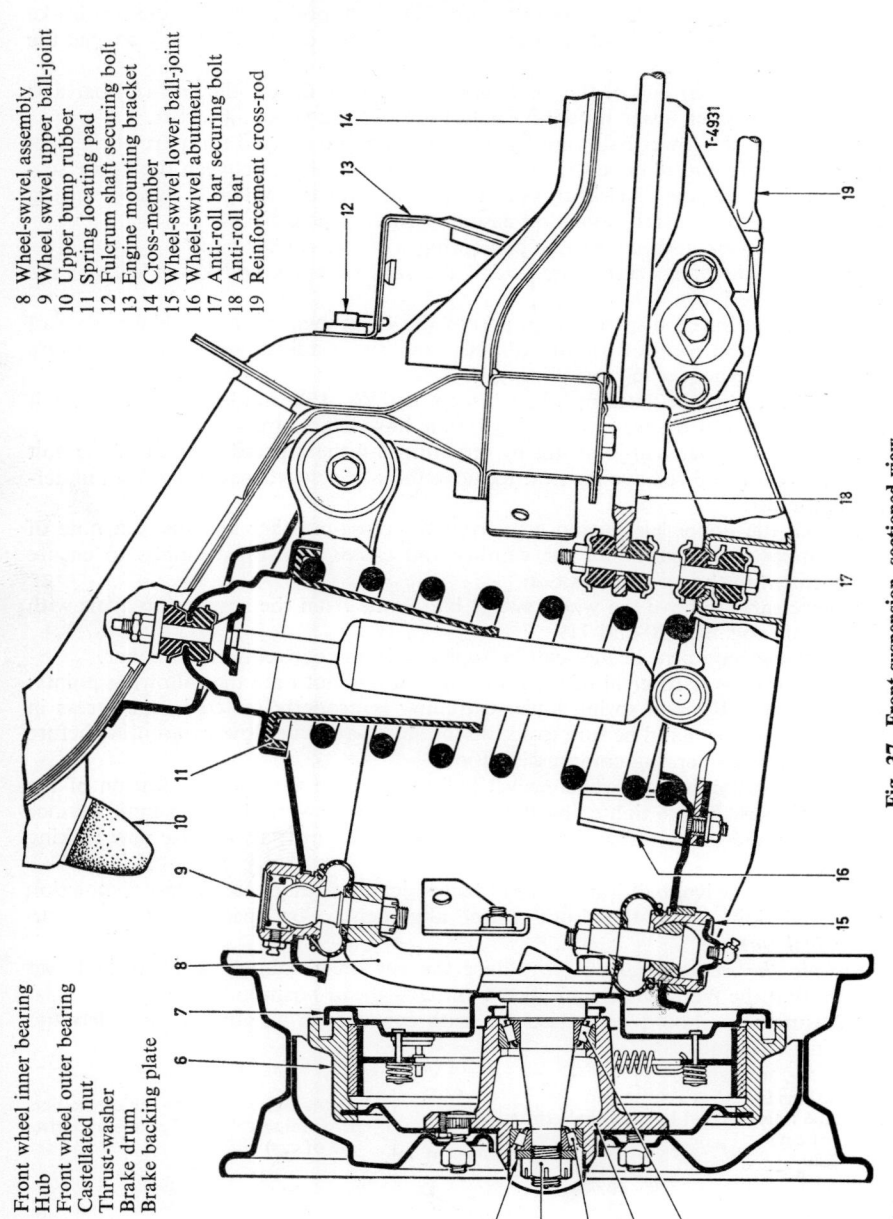

Fig. 37. Front suspension, sectioned view

Check and if necessary rectify front and rear tyre pressures.

The front end riding height is influenced by the condition of the rear springs, which should therefore be checked as follows:

Place a jack centrally under the front suspension cross-member and raise the car until the front wheels are both just clear of the ground. Front height irregularities are thereby prevented from influencing the rear end. Measure the vertical height from the ground to the centre of each rear spring rearmost shackle upper bolt; the riding heights should not differ more than 0·50 in; if necessary, eliminate the difference by placing a packing to the thickness of the difference beneath the tyre on the lowest side.

Remove the jack; bounce the front end of the car up and down several times, allowing the components to settle. Measure the vertical height from the ground to each lower suspension arm inner fulcrum shaft. The difference in height should not exceed the specified limits. No adjustment is possible, and if necessary install one or two new springs.

Front wheel alignment: For checking and adjustment of the front wheel alignment, the same preliminaries as detailed under 'Checking the riding height' should be carried out; only then may satisfactory results be obtained.

Check the front wheel bearing clearance and examine the steering ball-joints and bushes, etc., for wear or damage.

For dimensions, adjustments and tolerances see *Technical Data.*

Castor: The castor angle can be altered by adding or removing adjustment shims between the upper suspension arm fulcrum shaft and the chassis cross-member, or by adding or removing shims between the lower suspension arm fulcrum shaft and the cross-member.

First, commence adjustment at the upper suspension arm; the maximum number of adjustment shims fitted behind the fulcrum shaft amounts to six, including those for camber adjustment, whereas the difference in number of shims fitted at the front and the rear end of the shaft should not be greater than two.

Adding one shim to the front end or removing one from the rear end, increases the castor angle by $\frac{1}{2}°$; removing one shim from the front end or adding one to the rear end reduces the castor angle by $\frac{1}{2}°$.

Castor adjustment at the lower suspension arm fulcrum shaft is only allowed if the maximum permissible number of shims or the difference in the number of shims between the front end and rear end of the upper suspension arm does not give the castor angle needed.

By shimming at the lower suspension arm fulcrum shaft, adding one shim at the front and rear end of the shaft increases the castor angle by $\frac{3}{4}°$, whereas removing one shim from these points reduces the castor angle by $\frac{3}{4}°$. The maximum number of shims at each shaft end is two.

For the various models (in laden condition), the following specifications apply.

1964–1965	1966–1967
All models 1° 30′	All models 0° 30′ to 3° 15′

For the various 1966–67 models (in unladen condition) the following specifications are applicable:

FCS/D/D:	$\frac{1}{2}° - 3\frac{1}{4}°$
code 307*:	$0° - 3°$
FCH:	$\frac{1}{2}° - 3\frac{1}{4}°$
code 307*:	$0° - 3\frac{1}{2}°$

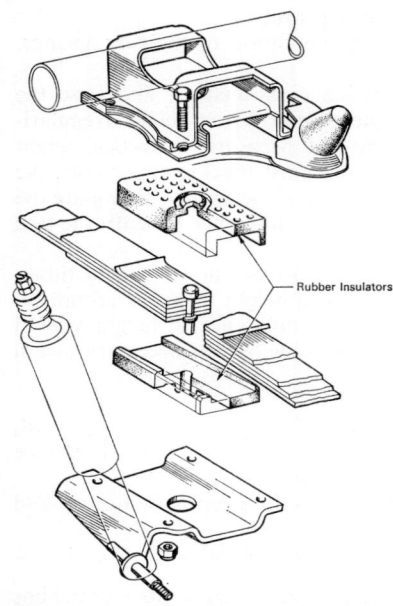

Rubber Insulators

Fig. 38. Rear suspension, axle attachment, exploded view showing rubber insulators

FCG: $0° - 3°$
   code 307*: $\frac{1}{2}° - 3\frac{1}{4}°$
FCW: $0° - 3°$
   code 307*: $1° - 3\frac{3}{4}°$
*These models have increased riding height.

Important: When removing an adjustment shim from the lower suspension arm rear attaching bolt, a camber adjustment shim should be added; when adding a shim to the rear attaching bolt of the lower suspension arm fulcrum shaft, a camber adjustment shim must be removed.

Camber: Camber adjustment is possible by adding or removing the relative adjustment shims between the lower suspension arm fulcrum shaft and the chassis cross-member; the total number of shims, including those for castor adjustment, should not be more than six. Never attempt to adjust the camber without first having checked and, if necessary, corrected, the castor angle.

Adding one camber adjustment shim increases camber by $\frac{1}{4}°$, whereas removing one shim reduces camber by $\frac{1}{4}°$.

For the various models (in laden condition) the following specifications are applicable:

1964–1965	1966–1967
For all models: $1° \ 30'$	For all models: $0° \ 15'$ to $1° \ 20'$

For all 1966–67 models (in unladen condition): $30'–1° \ 45'$

Steering axis inclination (S.A.I. or K.P.I.): The steering axis inclination cannot be altered; it is affected, however, by the camber adjustment and should amount to $5°15'$ to $6°15'$. If excessive deviation from this specification is observed, thoroughly check the wheel swivel assembly for distortion, etc.

Toe-in, checking and adjustment: Make sure that the front wheel on the driver's side is in the dead straight-ahead position; if this condition is obtained, the distance between the inner wheel rim and the centre of the lower suspension arm fulcrum shaft should be $14 \cdot 18$ in, measured in the horizontal plane.

If necessary this condition should be obtained by lengthening or shortening the driver's side tie-rod to the required degree. Then check and if necessary adjust the overall toe-in; if correction is necessary, this should be effected only by turning the opposite tie-rod. The requisite degree of toe-in for all models amounts to $0 \cdot 18$ in, measured at a diameter of 24 in.

Toe-out on turns: With the inner front wheel turned through $20°$, the outer wheel should be at $20°45'$ to $22°15'$.

If these limits are exceeded, examine the steering swivel arms for distortion.

Rear suspension: The rear wheel suspension employs semi-elliptical wide leaf-type springs and double-acting telescopic shock-absorbers. Improved lateral stability is a result of the non-parallel leaf springs, to which the rear axle is secured offset towards the front. The spring eyes and shackles are rubber-bushed and rubber pads insulate the axle attachment from the frame members.

The spring upper insulator retainer is welded to the rear axle tube; the spring is located in the spring seat, between two insulation pads, by the spring and the shock-absorber mounting plate, which is attached to the spring seat by four bolts and nuts.

Shock-absorbers: The front and rear shock-absorbers cannot be serviced; defective units should be replaced by new ones. When installing shock-absorbers, tighten the mounting nuts until they reach the end of the threads on the mounting bolts.

The shock-absorber action can be tested when comparing them with new units; however, do not forget that new shock-absorbers may have a greater resistance which will soon disappear when they are 'run-in.'

The front and rear shock-absorbers cannot be interchanged. The front shock-absorber effective stroke is 4–5 inches, the rear shock-absorbers have an effective stroke of 7 inches.

Wheel hubs and bearings: The front wheel hubs run on two adjustable tapered roller bearings of unequal diameter; the hub forms an integral unit with the brake drum or brake disc respectively. The rear wheels run on non-adjustable ball-bearings with built-in oil seals, where as on FCW and FCG models a heavier ball-bearing and a separate oil-seal is used.

For directions regarding replacement of a rear wheel bearing refer to 'Rear axle/ Differential' on page 51.

Checking and adjustment of front wheel bearing clearance: Jack-up the front of the car and ensure that the wheel in question is well clear of the ground; ensure that the brake shoes are not in contact with the brake drum. Shake the wheel vigorously and ensure that no excessive clearance is evident.

Make sure that any clearance is not caused by looseness of the front wheel swivel lower ball-joint; if necessary, eliminate clearance at this point by inserting a suitable bar between the suspension arm and the wheel swivel proper.

Adjust the wheel bearings as follows:

Remove the road wheel, the hub cap and the split-pin. With the aid of a box spanner tighten the hub nut; then back-off the nut and again tighten it, but this time by hand only. If necessary, back-off the nut to the required degree in order to align its slot with the split-pin hole, and install a new split-pin. Never tighten the nut to align with the hole.

Steering gear: The steering box is of the recirculating ball type. The worm shaft runs in two ball-bearings, the end-float is adjusted by shims fitted beneath the steering box bottom cover. The Pitman shaft reaction is taken at its upper end by a spring-loaded ball-bearing. The light metal housing is riveted to the steering column, the steering box must therefore be removed with the steering column.

Removal of the steering unit: Remove the parcel shelf and withdraw the steering wheel. Detach the steering column cover plates and remove the direction-indicator switch.

Remove the dash panel in order to gain access to the steering column upper support nut, and remove same.

On cars fitted with a steering column lock, disconnect the combined ignition and starter switch multi-connector plug.

Unhook the clutch and brake pedal return springs from the steering column lower support. On models with a three-speed gearbox slacken the gearshift lever to the lower end of the operating shaft locating bolt, then withdraw the gearshift lever.

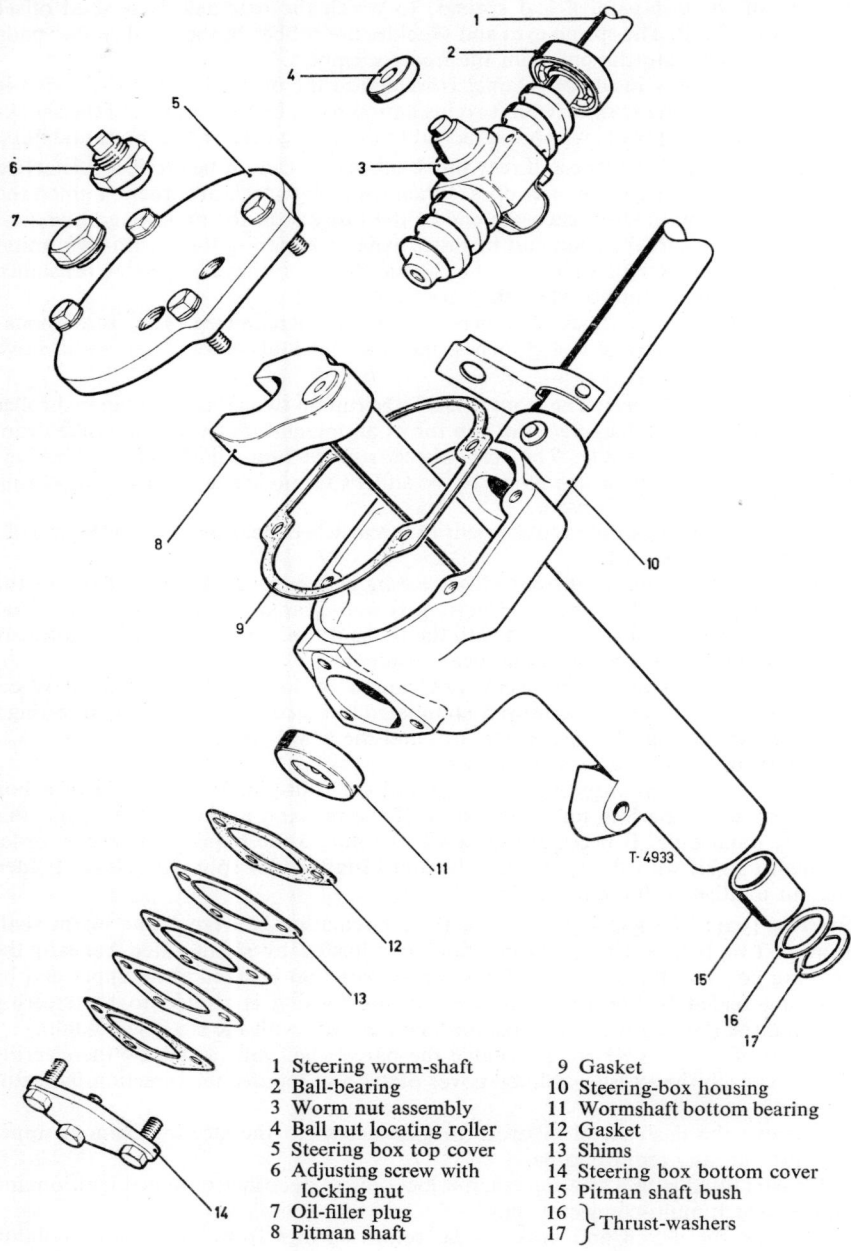

T· 4933

1 Steering worm-shaft
2 Ball-bearing
3 Worm nut assembly
4 Ball nut locating roller
5 Steering box top cover
6 Adjusting screw with
     locking nut
7 Oil-filler plug
8 Pitman shaft

9 Gasket
10 Steering-box housing
11 Wormshaft bottom bearing
12 Gasket
13 Shims
14 Steering box bottom cover
15 Pitman shaft bush
16 ⎫
17 ⎬ Thrust-washers

Fig. 39. Steering gear, exploded view

Slacken-off the clamping bolt securing the gearshift lever guide to the upper end of the steering column, then withdraw the guide and the operating shaft.

Detach the lower end of the clutch relay lever interconnecting rod.

Remove the brake and clutch pedals together with their support.

Remove the toe board and clutch linkage covers, and remove the clutch relay rod.

Detach the clutch relay lever support from the steering column.

Remove the pitman arm from its shaft.

On three-speed models, disconnect the selector rod lever from the cross-shaft forked end and withdraw the rod from its bush in the bottom of the steering box. Disconnect the control rod. Remove the steering-housing-to-engine-mounting-side rail securing bolts.

Remove the steering column upper support and withdraw the steering unit.

Installation of the steering unit: Installation is a direct reversal of the removal procedure, noting the following:

Initially do not fully tighten the steering box securing bolts; first, fully tighten the steering column upper support and finally fully tighten the steering box bolts; this sequence is important to avoid any pre-load or tension on the steering column. Ensure that the selector shaft engages the guide bushing on the steering box.

Dismantling the steering box: With the aid of a screwdriver, prise out the steering shaft bearing. If a steering column lock is fitted, remove the cheese-headed screws and drill out the two break-head screws. This is essential in order to release the lock housing from its locating dowel on the column.

Remove the toe-board aperture cover, slacken the pitman shaft adjusting lock nut and screw.

Remove the steering box cover and main nut roller.

Drain the oil and withdraw the pitman shaft.

Remove the steering box bottom cover, the shims and the gaskets.

Push out the worm shaft lower bearing outer race and the balls.

Screw the main worm nut off the worm and withdraw the latter with the shaft through the bottom aperture.

Remove the main nut assembly and the upper bearing and balls from the housing.

Separate the retainer and ball transfer tube from the main nut.

If necessary, remove the pitman shaft oil-seal; this can be done after tapping back the staking lock and removing the retaining washer.

Carefully clean and inspect all parts, replacing those that are worn or damaged.

Assembly and adjustment: Lubricate the worm-shaft bearing with the recommended grease and dip the bearing felt in clean oil. When installed, the bearing outer race flange should contact the top of the column.

After installing a new pitman shaft oil-seal and retaining washer, stake the end of the bore at four places to secure the oil-seal retaining washer.

Make sure that the balls run freely through the transfer tube on the worm nut.

Smear the worm-shaft bearing races with petroleum jelly to retain the bearing balls in position.

Fit the bottom cover with the adjustment shims and new gaskets.

Prior to installing the pitman shaft, adjust the worm-shaft bearing pre-load to the specified limits by adding or removing shims at the bottom cover.

Before checking the worm-shaft bearing pre-load, temporarily install the steering wheel, the nut roller and the cover with a new gasket to prevent the main nut jamming against the housing. To the rim of the steering wheel attach a spring balance and rotate the wheel; this should require a force of between 2 to 8 oz.

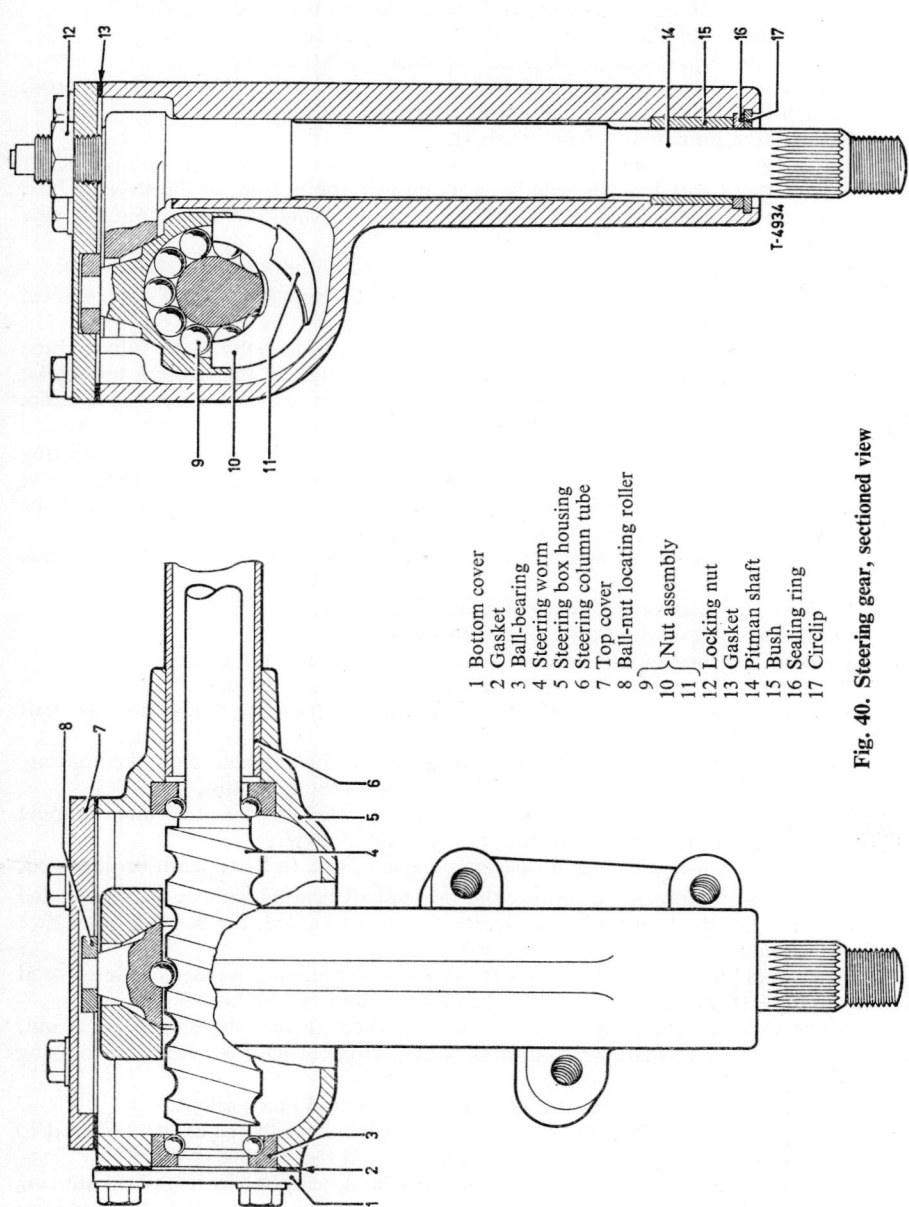

T-4934

1 Bottom cover
2 Gasket
3 Ball-bearing
4 Steering worm
5 Steering box housing
6 Steering column tube
7 Top cover
8 Ball-nut locating roller
9
10 } Nut assembly
11
12 Locking nut
13 Gasket
14 Pitman shaft
15 Bush
16 Sealing ring
17 Circlip

Fig. 40. Steering gear, sectioned view

Dimensions in inches
1   1.90
2   4.56
3   2.74
4   2.06
5   1.10
6   5.20
7   2.65
8   1.80
9   5.20
A   Steering arm
B   Swivel assembly
C   Pitman arm
D   Steering idler arm

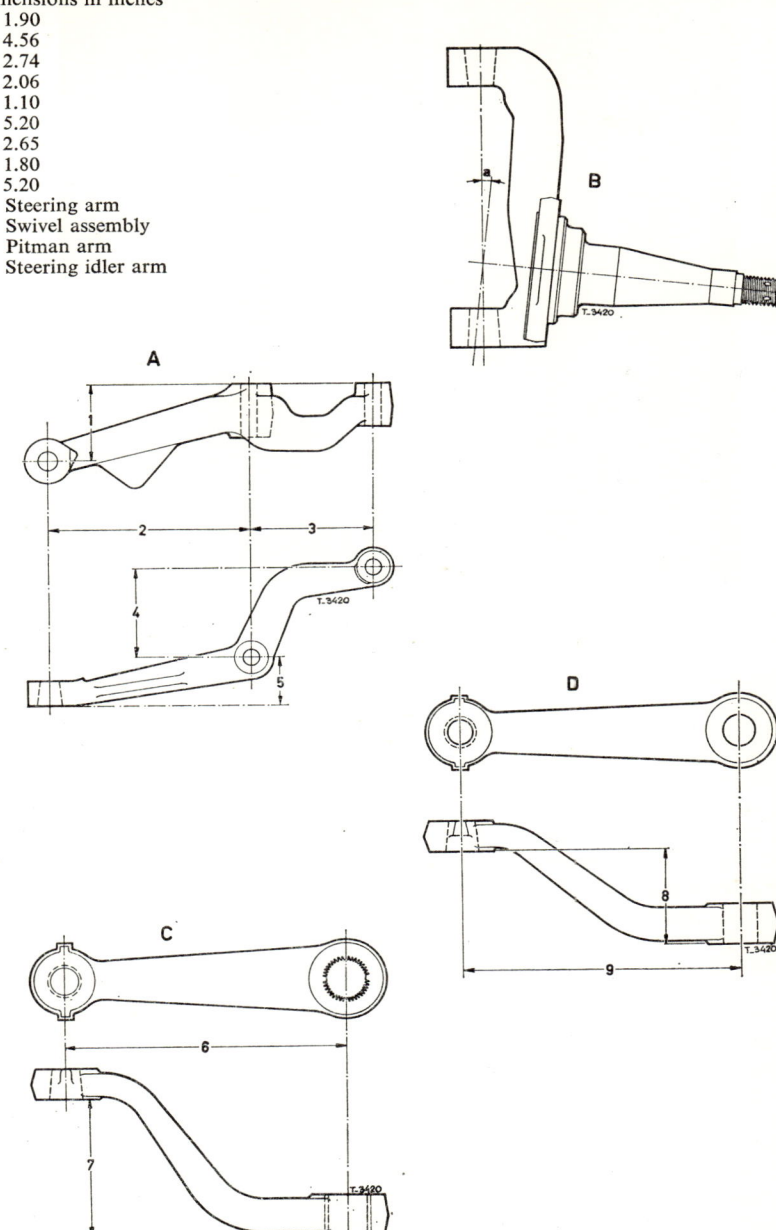

Fig. 41. Steering arm and knuckle dimensions

Fig. 42. Disc brake, installed

Lubricate the pitman shaft bush with oil and insert the shaft; engage the shaft with the main nut as follows:

Install the nut roller and the cover with its gasket and fully tighten the cover bolts.

Set the steering wheel in the dead straight position (half of its total travel).

Screw in the pitman shaft adjusting screw until it contacts the shaft; then tighten the locknut. Attach a spring balance to the steering wheel as described above and check the force to rotate the wheel through an angle of approximately 30° to either side of the straight-ahead position, which should be between 12 to 16 oz.

If the force required is beyond these limits, turn the adjusting screw as necessary. When the requisite overall pre-load is within the specified limits do not forget to tighten the locknut; then remove the steering wheel.

Install the direction-indicator switch and complete the assembly as a reversal of the dismantling operation.

When the unit is installed in the vehicle, do not forget to fill the steering box with the recommended lubricant.

Steering idler arm removal and dismantling: Jack-up the front end of the car and support on chassis stands.

Remove the bottom nut locating the tie-rod on the idler arm.

Remove the bolts and idler arm housing bracket to engine mount side rail securing plate. Detach the idler arm from the tie-rod.

If necessary, extract the stud from the idler arm with tool Z.8510.

Remove the nut and the plain and nylon washers.

Withdraw the idler arm with the shaft from the housing. It is not recommended that the idler arm be removed from its shaft.

Thoroughly clean and inspect all parts, replacing any that are worn, damaged or distorted.

Assembly and installation: Clamp the idler-arm housing in a vice and coat the bore of the idler-arm shaft bearing bush with the recommended grease, making sure that the indentations in the bush are completely filled.

Insert the idler arm into the housing; ensure that the nylon thrust-washers fitted to both ends of the housing are in their original position on the shaft. Install the plain washer, followed by the castellated nut. Fully tighten the nut, and with the aid of a spring balance, check the force required to rotate the idler arm; this should be 3 lb. If the load is beyond this limit, correct by pressing the idler arm towards or away from the housing as necessary.

Finally, install the idler arm retaining circlip, ensuring that it is properly lodged in its groove.

Install the assembly as a reversal of the removal operations.

Tighten the housing securing bolts to 25 lb ft.

Brake system: The foot brake hydraulically operates the front and rear wheel brakes; at the front two leading shoe drum brakes are fitted, at the rear leading/trailing shoe drum brakes are used, whereas on VX 4/90 models the front wheel brakes are of the vacuum servo-assisted disc type and the rear brakes are of the duo-servo drum type. Front disc brakes and vacuum servo power brake units are available on other models as an optional extra.

The front wheel drum type brakes are automatically adjusting and are fitted with two single-ended hydraulic slave cylinders, each actuating one shoe. The leading/trailing shoe type rear brakes are operated by a single-ended floating type slave cylinder.

The parking brake operates mechanically on both rear brakes only.

The pendant-type foot-brake pedal pivots on nylon bushes and is connected to the brake master cylinder by means of a push-rod. The brake pedal free travel is pre-set in production and should not require adjustment.

The master cylinder, with integral brake fluid reservoir, is of the centre valve type and is secured to the brake pedal support.

Disc brakes: Girling disc brakes are comprised of a caliper unit in two parts, each half with one brake cylinder bore. The brake pads are automatically adjusting and do not require periodic attention other than checking their thickness and replacing when necessary. The minimum thickness for brake pads is 0·12 in; if the pads wear beyond this limit, heat will be transmitted to the brake fluid in the caliper causing vaporization.

Brake pad renewal: Remove the front wheel and syphon sufficient brake fluid from the master cylinder brake fluid reservoir to allow a rise of fluid level when the caliper pistons are forced back into their cylinders by applying pressure by hand.

Remove the spring clips from the brake-pad retaining pins and withdraw the pins, the brake pads and the anti-squeal shims from the caliper.

NOTE: *Never depress the brake pedal when the brake pads are removed.*

Install the new brake pads and the anti-squeal shims, ensuring that the arrow on each shim is pointing in the direction of forward rotation of the disc, then insert the pins and spring clips.

Depress the brake pedal several times to re-position the pistons in the caliper unit and top-up the brake fluid reservoir with the recommended type of brake fluid to within 0·30 in from the top. Re-fit the road wheel.

NOTE: *Pads and linings should be replaced on both the front wheel brakes or both*

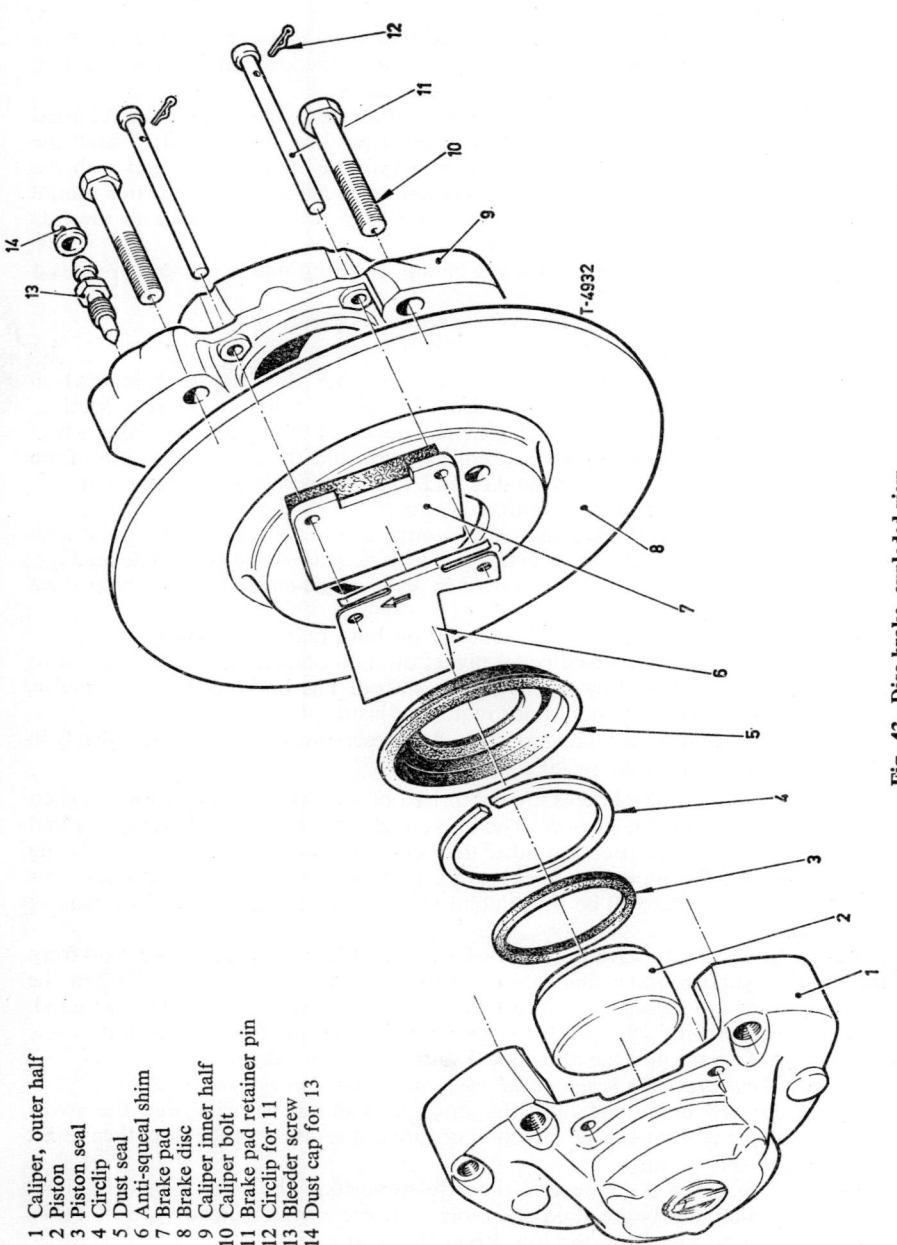

T-4932

1 Caliper, outer half
2 Piston
3 Piston seal
4 Circlip
5 Dust seal
6 Anti-squeal shim
7 Brake pad
8 Brake disc
9 Caliper inner half
10 Caliper bolt
11 Brake pad retainer pin
12 Circlip for 11
13 Bleeder screw
14 Dust cap for 13

Fig. 43. Disc brake, exploded view

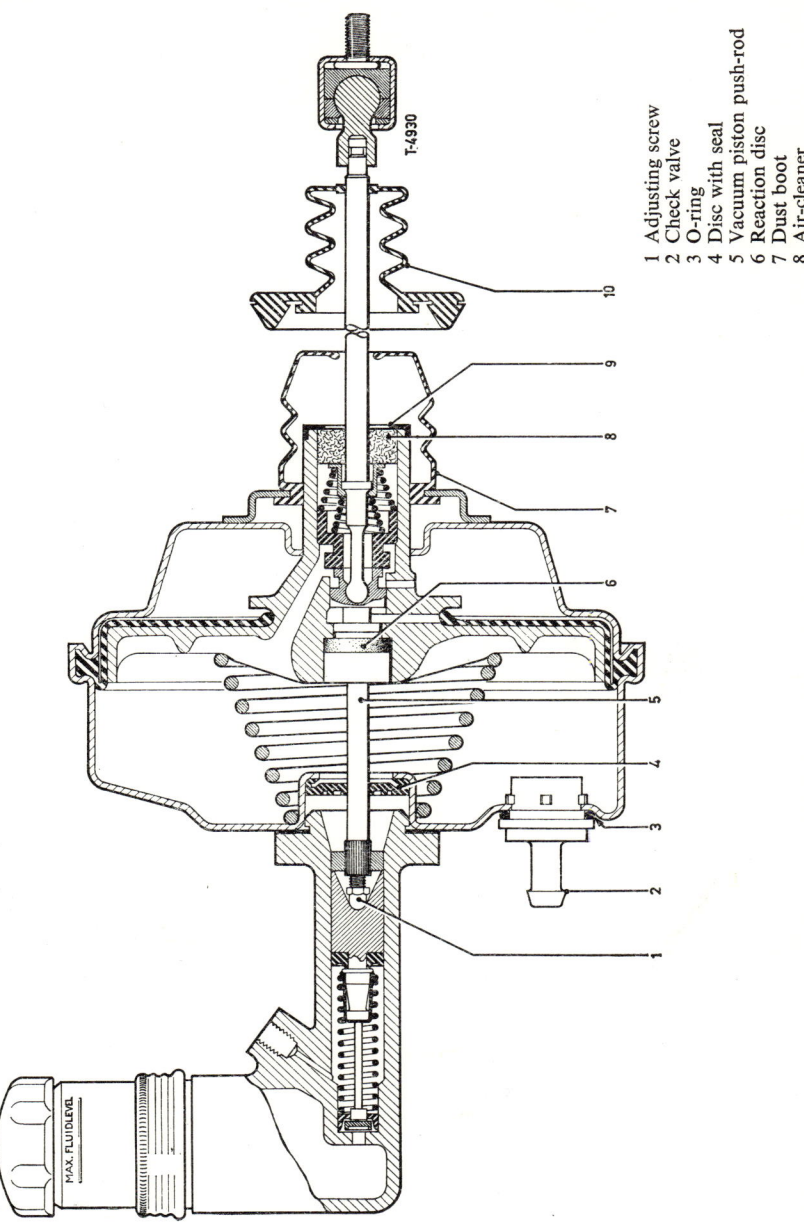

1 Adjusting screw
2 Check valve
3 O-ring
4 Disc with seal
5 Vacuum piston push-rod
6 Reaction disc
7 Dust boot
8 Air-cleaner
9 Cap
10 Dust boot

T-4930

Fig. 44. Vacuum servo unit, sectioned view

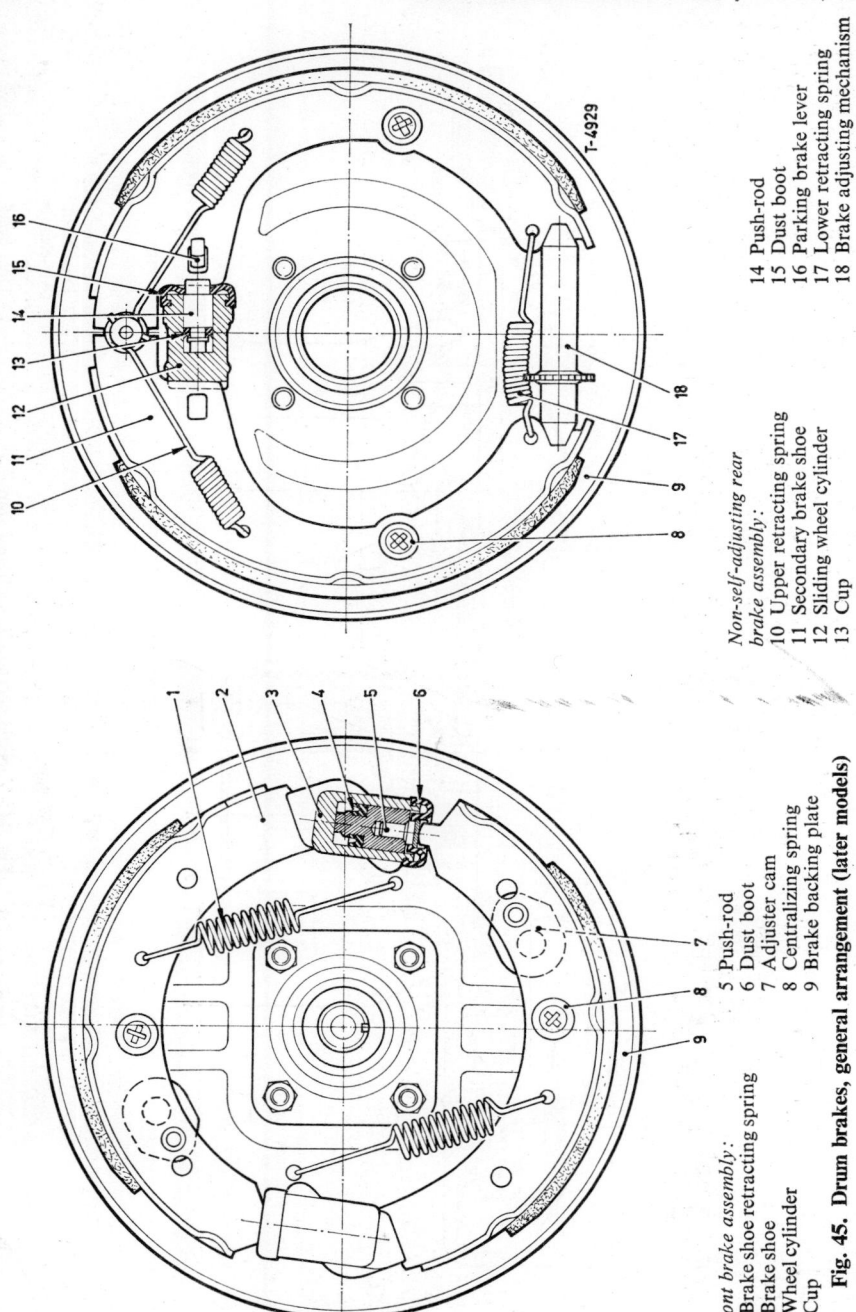

T-4929

14 Push-rod
15 Dust boot
16 Parking brake lever
17 Lower retracting spring
18 Brake adjusting mechanism

*Non-self-adjusting rear
brake assembly:*
10 Upper retracting spring
11 Secondary brake shoe
12 Sliding wheel cylinder
13 Cup

Front brake assembly:
1 Brake shoe retracting spring
2 Brake shoe
3 Wheel cylinder
4 Cup

5 Push-rod
6 Dust boot
7 Adjuster cam
8 Centralizing spring
9 Brake backing plate

Fig. 45. Drum brakes, general arrangement (later models)

the rear wheel brakes to ensure balanced braking.

Removal and installation of a brake caliper: Jack-up the front of the car and remove the brake pads as described above.

Replace the brake fluid reservoir filler cap with one on which the vent hole has been sealed and disconnect the brake hose at the caliper.

Remove the bolts and lock washers securing the caliper to the front wheel swivel assembly and remove the caliper. If necessary, renew the piston sealing rings.

NOTE: *The two caliper halves should under no circumstances be separated.*

Installation is a reversal of the removal procedure. Always install new caliper attaching bolts, which must be tightened to a torque of 38 lb ft.

After installation do not forget to top-up the brake fluid reservoir and to replace the dummy filler cap with the original cap.

Brake vacuum servo unit: Cars equipped with disc brakes are power-assisted by means of a vacuum servo, which is connected to the engine inlet manifold so that with the engine running the necessary vacuum is created on one side of an operating piston in the vacuum chamber. When the brake pedal is actuated, air under atmospheric pressure is admitted into the chamber at the other side of the vacuum piston so that the piston will move toward the low-pressure region in the chamber. This movement of the vacuum piston is transmitted to the brake cylinder operating push-rod which provides greater stopping power with relatively little pedal pressure.

If the engine stalls or if the vacuum is unavailable for any other reason, the vacuum servo becomes inoperative; the unit, however, is constructed in such a manner that the pedal pressure is then transmitted directly to the brake master cylinder, making the system like any other non-power-assisted braking system, and increasing the physical effort required by the driver.

Removal and installation of the servo unit: Replace the brake fluid reservoir filler cap by one without a vent hole; disconnect the hydraulic pipe at the master cylinder, remove the securing nuts and withdraw the master cylinder complete. Disconnect the vacuum hose at the servo unit and detach the operating push-rod from the brake pedal. Release the dust boot round the pedal push-rod from the pedal floor section; release the servo unit from its bracket and remove the unit, together with the pedal push-rod.

Installation is a reversal of the above operation. Replace filler cap. If the servo unit has been dismantled, proceed as follows:

After installation of the unit on the vehicle, run the engine and check whether the vacuum push-rod properly seats against the reaction disc, thus preventing vacuum leakage. Screw the adjusting bolt out until it protrudes between 0·095 to 0·100 in from the servo unit. Switch off the engine and apply two drops of Loctite Sealant, Grade B, round the threads of the bolt adjacent to the push-rod. Install the brake master cylinder and bleed the hydraulic system.

Dismantling: If the vacuum servo should require attention on account of faulty operation, the only serviceable items are the air-filter, the hydraulic push-rod with adjusting bolt, plate and seal assembly, the reaction disc, the non-return valve and ring; if the trouble cannot be eliminated by replacing the above parts, the unit should be replaced, as further dismantling is not permissible.

Replacement of the above-mentioned parts is carried out as follows:

1 Pull back the dust boot, ease off the filter retainer and remove the air-filter.
2 Remove the hydraulic push-rod, the plate and seal, and remove the adjusting bolt from the rod.
3 Remove the reaction disc from the push-rod or diaphragm plate.

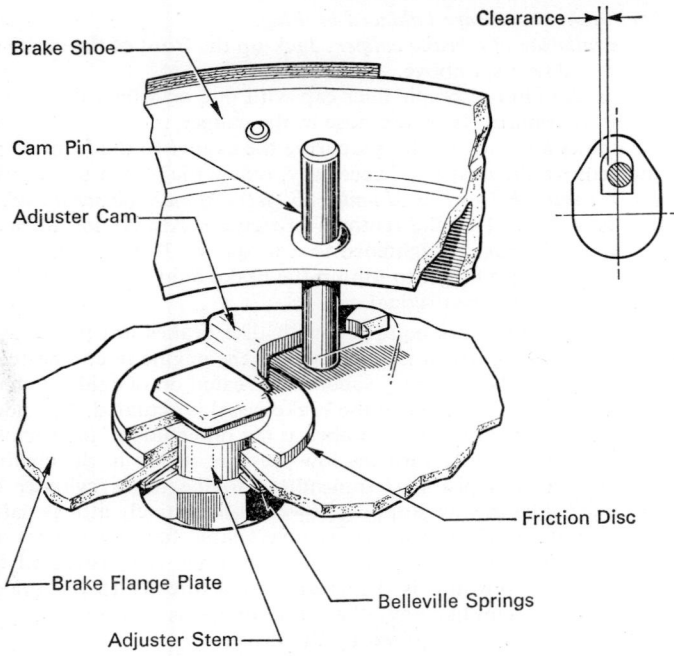

Fig. 46. Front drum brake, detail of automatic adjuster

4 Turn the non-return valve anti-clockwise by one quarter of a turn and withdraw the valve and O-ring.

When turning the valve, take care that the stop tags in the servo housing are not damaged.

Thoroughly clean and inspect all parts, replace those that are worn or damaged.
Assembly: Assembly is a reversal of the dismantling procedure.

When installing a new non-return valve, use a new O-ring.

Lubricate the reaction disc, the vacuum push-rod, the plate and seal with the recommended grease.

When assembling the adjusting bolt, do not tighten the bolt.

Drum brakes: The front drum brakes are each fitted with two single-acting slave cylinders and two adjusting cams, whereas the rear brakes have one single-acting slave cylinder and one adjusting cam. The front wheel brakes are a matched set with their respective brake drums, therefore these parts should not be interchanged or replaced separately. The front brakes are of the self-adjusting type; the rear brakes on earlier models are also self-adjusting.

Foot brake and parking brake adjustment: The front wheel brakes (drum type or disc type) are self-adjusting and do not require adjustment. Rear brakes of the non-self-adjusting type are adjusted as follows: Jack-up the rear end of the car and check that the parking brake is fully released. From the brake backing plate remove the dust shield and with the aid of a suitable lever or screwdriver, rotate the adjuster star wheel until the wheel is completely locked; then back-off the adjuster two

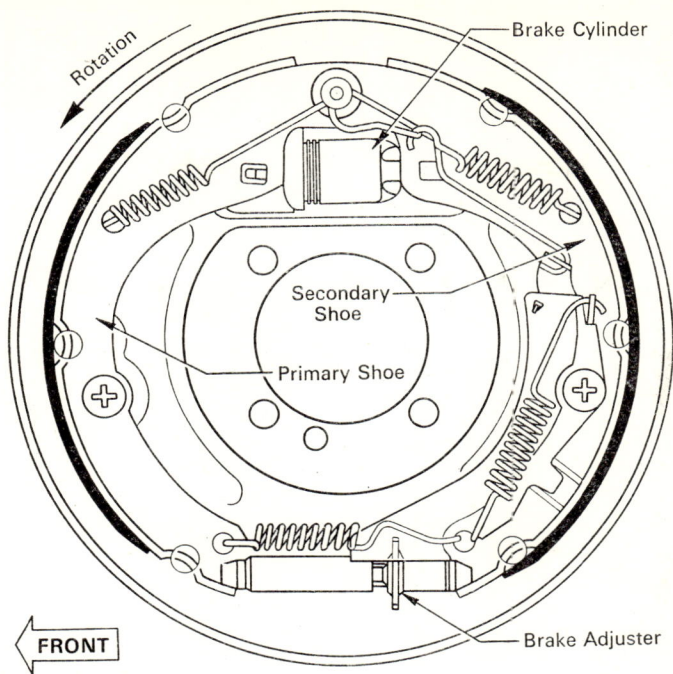

Fig. 47. Rear brake, early models, general arrangement

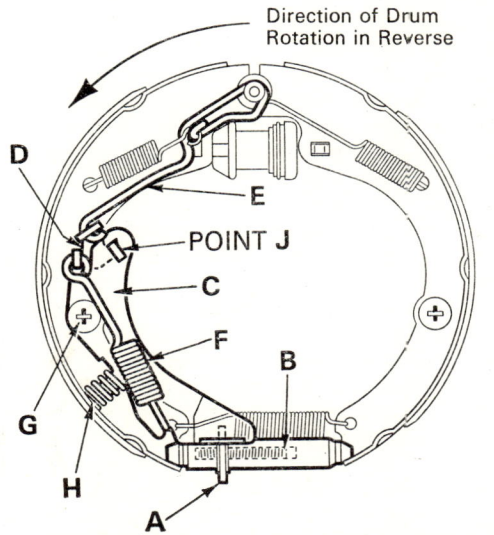

Fig. 48. Rear brake, early models, adjuster mechanism

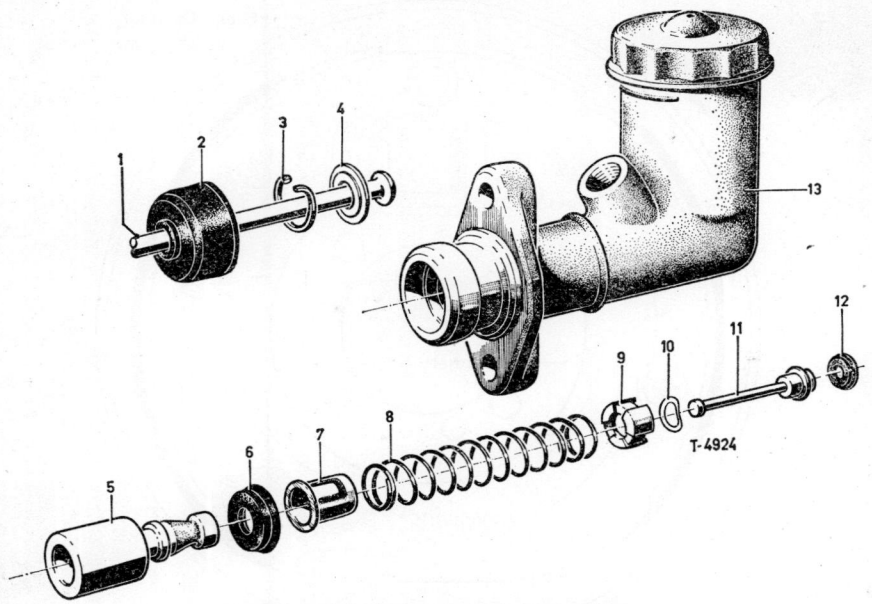

Fig. 49. Brake master cylinder, exploded view

1 Push-rod	4 Push-rod abutment	7 Spring guide	11 Valve stem
2 Dust boot	washer	8 Spring	12 Valve
3 Circlip	5 Piston	9 Spacer	13 Brake master
	6 Cup	10 Waved washer	cylinder

notches until the wheel rotates freely. Finally, install the dust shield. Repeat this procedure for the other rear brake.

For brake pedal free travel adjustment see *Brake master cylinder.*

The parking brake is automatically adjusted when adjusting the rear brakes; if, however, the parking brake operating cable is stretched too far, adjustment is effected as follows: Disconnect the front cable and adjust the rear brakes as described above, then adjust the rear cable by connecting it to both operating levers in such a manner that the distance between the front cable clevis pin centre-line and the final drive housing amounts to approximately 2·36 in; for this purpose the operating levers are provided with several holes at different radii.

Now adjust the front cable to eliminate all slack without causing the brakes to rub, tighten the locknut at the adjuster fork and connect the fork to the central lever. The brakes should be hard on when the parking brake lever is pulled up about 10 notches; on VX 4/90 models about four notches.

Self-adjusting rear brakes (early models): Prior to chassis number 5047973 (April 1965) the rear brakes were provided with automatic adjustment mechanisms, whereby adjustment takes place at every brake application when the car moves backwards.

The principle of operation is as follows (see Fig. 48).

The adjuster is operated by the shoe, which acts as primary shoe in the reverse direction of vehicle motion (i.e., the left-hand shoe in Fig. 48). Adjustment is effected by means of the toothed wheel (A) which is integral with one half of the screwed link (B). The automatic adjustment mechanism consists basically of three links: C, D and E in the diagram, which are connected together as shown. Under normal operation, links C and D are held together under the action of spring F, and function as one unit. Link C is attached to the brake shoe web through a spring-loaded pivot at G, and one end of the link engages the teeth of the adjuster wheel.

When a brake application is made in reverse, the brake assembly rotates in an anti-clockwise direction relative to the back plate and the shoe adjustment pin. The link E pulling on link D causes D and C to rotate about point G, against the action of spring H, so that the end of lever C causes the adjusting wheel to rotate. This effects an extension of the screwed link (B) whenever the clearance of the brake linings from the drum is greater than that equivalent to the distance from one adjusting wheel tooth to the next.

When, however, a heavy brake application is made, the high axial load in the screwed link (B) prevents, through friction at the threads, turning of the adjusting wheel. If links C and E were directly connected, this would result in very high stresses in these parts and consequent damage or over-stressing. The function of link D is to prevent this happening. When the adjusting wheel is stopped by friction from rotating, extension of spring F takes place, allowing link D to rotate relative to link C about point J. Link D thus acts as an unloading device and relieves the stresses in link C.

Hand adjustment of the lining clearance is also possible if occasion arises after removing a small metal cover from an access hole in the back plate.

Brake master cylinder: The brake master cylinder is mounted on the scuttle, forward of the brake pedal, and has an integral brake fluid reservoir. The reservoir should be filled with the recommended lubricant until the fluid level reaches to $0 \cdot 30$ in below the rim of the filler plug hole. The brake fluid enters the master cylinder via a non-return or check valve. The brake pedal free travel cannot be adjusted as it is determined by the operating push-rod of fixed length.

BODY

Front door lock, *removal and installation:* From each door handle remove the Phillips-headed retaining screw, withdraw the handles and remove the plastic wear ring. Note the position of the handles, to ensure correct replacement.

Remove the armrest and unscrew the door locking plunger.

Carefully remove the door trim panel and the water deflector, the glued edges of which should be eased off with a knife or similar sharp instrument.

Ensure that the window is in its topmost position and remove the door lock remote control securing screws; unhook the mechanism from the remote control rod and remove. From the lock side of the door remove the two window guide bracket securing screws and detach the bracket from the guide.

Remove the door lock securing screws and manoeuvre the lock mechanism so that it unhooks from the push-button mechanism of the exterior door handle, and withdraw the assembly, together with the remote control rod, through the aperture in the door panel. If required, remove the outer door handle.

Installation is a reversal of the removal procedure.

Lubricate the lock and other pivot points with high melting point grease.

Ensure that when the lock lever is against its lower abutment, a minimum clearance exists between the lever and the push-button pin. If necessary, release the lock, disconnect the actuating rod from the lever and select one of the other two holes in the lever to obtain this condition. With the push-button fully depressed, the lock lever must be in contact with the upper stop on the lock plate.

Vent pane, *removal and installation:* Remove the door trim panel as detailed for the previous operation. Remove the window bottom stop as well as the anti-rattle bracket situated directly below the window stop.

Lower the window fully and release the weather strip from the outer panel (four clips); remove the strip.

Remove the three screws securing the vent pane assembly to the door frame as well as those securing the glass guide to the door inner panel, and remove the vent pane, together with the glass guide upward of the door.

Installation is a reversal of the removal procedure.

When securing the glass guide, do not tighten the lowest screw fully until the guide has been adjusted so that the window can freely slide up and down.

Window winding mechanism, front and rear:

Removal and installation:

Remove the door trim panelling as detailed under *Front door lock, removal and installation,* on page 77.

Raise the window fully, support it from below and remove the winding mechanism securing screws. Detach the arm from the glass support channel. Remove the mechanism through the panel lower aperture. For removal of the window glass only, it is not necessary to remove the winding mechanism but proceed as follows:

Remove the vent pane as described previously and slide the regulator arm out of the glass support channel by moving the glass towards the front. Remove the window through the top of the door.

A rear door window is removed as follows:

Fully lower the glass after having removed the bottom stop and the anti-rattle bracket. Remove the window guide securing screws and move the guide forward; push the rear of the glass downward and remove the window guide. Remove the fixed rear quarter window and pull the rear of the glass upward and towards the rear to slide the regulator arm out of the glass support guide. Remove the glass through the top of the door.

Installation is effected as a reversal of the above operations; see also the instructions given under *Removal and installation of a vent pane.*

Rear door lock, *removal and installation:* Remove the door trim panel as detailed on page 77 and remove the outside door handle, which is similar to the front door outer handles. Disconnect both operating rods at the lock, remove the lock securing screws and withdraw the lock from the door.

Installation is a reversal of the removal procedure.

ELECTRICAL EQUIPMENT

Electrical system: 12 volts, positive earth connection (1967 models: negative earth). For wiring diagrams refer to Figs. 50 and 51.

Generator: Two-brush, two-pole, shunt-type generator, comprising an armature, field magnet system and brush gear, in a yoke with two detachable bearing covers.

The drive end of the armature runs on a replaceable ball-bearing whereas the commutator end of the shaft runs in a replaceable sintered bronze bearing bush.

Dismantling: After removal, the generator can be dismantled as follows: Unscrew the pulley nut, remove the lock washer and extract the pulley; take care not to lose the Woodruff key.

Remove both generator through-bolts and withdraw the commutator end bearing cover; if necessary, loosen the cover by tapping with a soft hammer.

Remove the pulley-end bearing cover together with the armature, taking care not to lose the fibre thrust washer fitted to the pulley-end of the armature shaft.

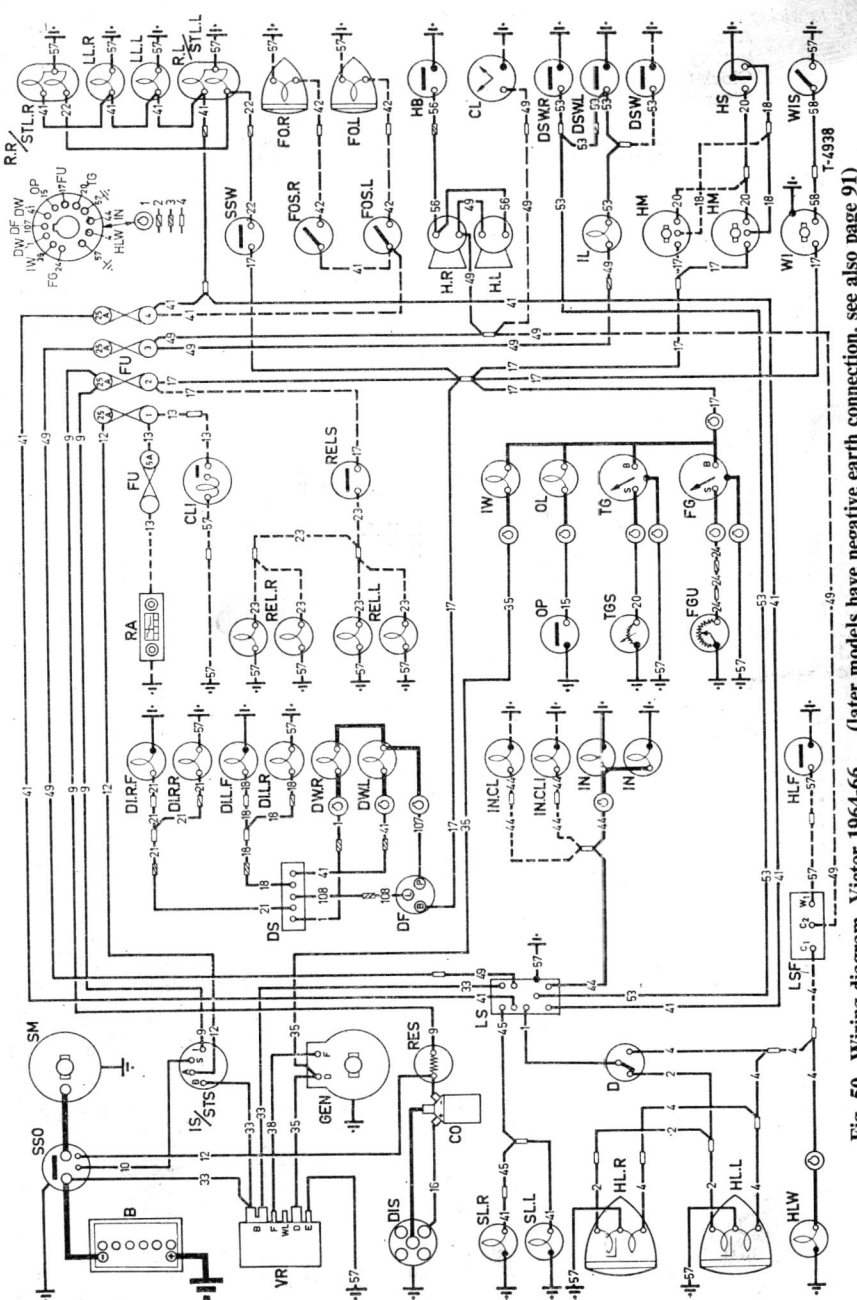

Fig. 50. Wiring diagram, Victor 1964-66   (later models have negative earth connection, see also page 91)

Key to wiring diagrams, Figs. 50 *and* 51:

A	Ammeter (FCH only)	IN	Instrument light
B	Battery	IN.CL	Clock light (if fitted)
CL	Clock (optional extra)	IN.CLI	Cigar lighter light (if fitted)
CLI	Cigar lighter (optional extra)	IN.RC	Tachometer light (FCH only)
COR	Coil resistor	IN.TG/OG	Temperature and oil pressure
D	Dimmer switch		gauge light
DF	Direction-indicator flasher	IN.SPM	Speedometer light
DI.L.F	Direction-indicator, left front	IN.A/FG	Ammeter (if fitted) and fuel
DI.L.R	Direction-indicator, left rear		gauge light
DI.R.F	Direction-indicator, right front	IS/STS	Ignition/starter switch
DI.R.R	Direction-indicator, right rear	IW	Ignition warning light
DIS	Distributor	LL.L	Number-plate lamp, left
DS	Direction-indicator switch	LL.R	Number-plate lamp, right
DSW.L	Door switch, left	LS	Light switch, with combined
DSW.R	Door switch, right		instrument light rheostat and
DSW	Door switch, rear (estate cars		built-in terminal circuit-breaker
	only)	LSF	Headlamp flasher unit (if fitted)
DW.L	Direction-indicator warning light,	OL	Oil pressure warning light
	left		(not on FCH)
DW.R	Direction-indicator warning light,	OP	Oil pressure sender unit
	right		(not on FCH)
FG	Fuel gauge	R.L/STL.L	Rear lamp/stop lamp, left
FGU	Fuel tank gauge unit	R.R/STL.R	Rear lamp/stop lamp, right
FO.L	Fog lamp, left	RA	Radio
FO.R	Fog lamp, right	REL.L	Reversing lamp, left
FOS.L	Fog lamp switch, left	REL.R	Reversing lamp, right
FOS.R	Fog lamp switch, right	RELS	Reversing lamp switch
FU	Fuses	SL.L	Sidelamp, left
GEN	Generator	SL.R	Sidelamp, right
H.L	Horn, left	SM	Starter motor
H.R	Horn, right	SSO	Starter motor solenoid
HB	Horn ring	SSW	Stop lamp switch
HL.L	Headlamp, left	TG	Temperature gauge
HL.R	Headlamp, right	TGS	Temperature gauge sender unit
HLF	Headlamp flasher (if fitted)	VR	Voltage regulator
HLW	High beam warning light	WI	Windscreen-wiper
HM	Heater motor	WIS	Windscreen-wiper switch
HS	Heater motor switch		
IL	Interior light		

FO.L Fog lamp, left / FO.R Fog lamp, right / FOS.L Fog lamp switch, left / FOS.R Fog lamp switch, right } (if fitted)

REL.L Reversing lamp, left / REL.R Reversing lamp, right / RELS Reversing lamp switch } (optional extra)

NOTE: *Bold printed lines in diagram represent printed wiring*

Key to wire colours (Figs. 50 *and* 51):

1	Blue	16	White/black	33	Brown	49	Purple
2	Blue/red	17	Green	35	Brown/yellow	53	Purple/white
4	Blue/white	18	Green/red	37	Brown/white	56	Purple/black
9	White	20	Green/blue	38	Brown/green	57	Black
10	White/red	21	Green/white	41	Red	58	Black/red
12	White/blue	22	Green/purple	42	Red/yellow	107	Light green/purple
13	White/green	23	Green/brown	44	Red/white	108	Light green/brown
15	White/brown	24	Green/black	45	Red/green		

As all necessary armature testing can be carried out with the pulley-end bearing cover fitted, it is not necessary to remove the bearing cover, unless, of course, the ball-bearing should need replacing or the commutator needs re-machining. If necessary, remove the field coil assemblies from the yoke; this operation requires the use of a wheel-operated screwdriver.

Carefully clean all parts with suitable solvent but only use the cleaning agent sparingly. Refrain from using any cleaning liquid on the field coil assemblies.

If required, the commutator-end bearing bush can be replaced provided that the special tools for this operation are available.

Before installation the porous bronze bush must be saturated with engine oil as follows:

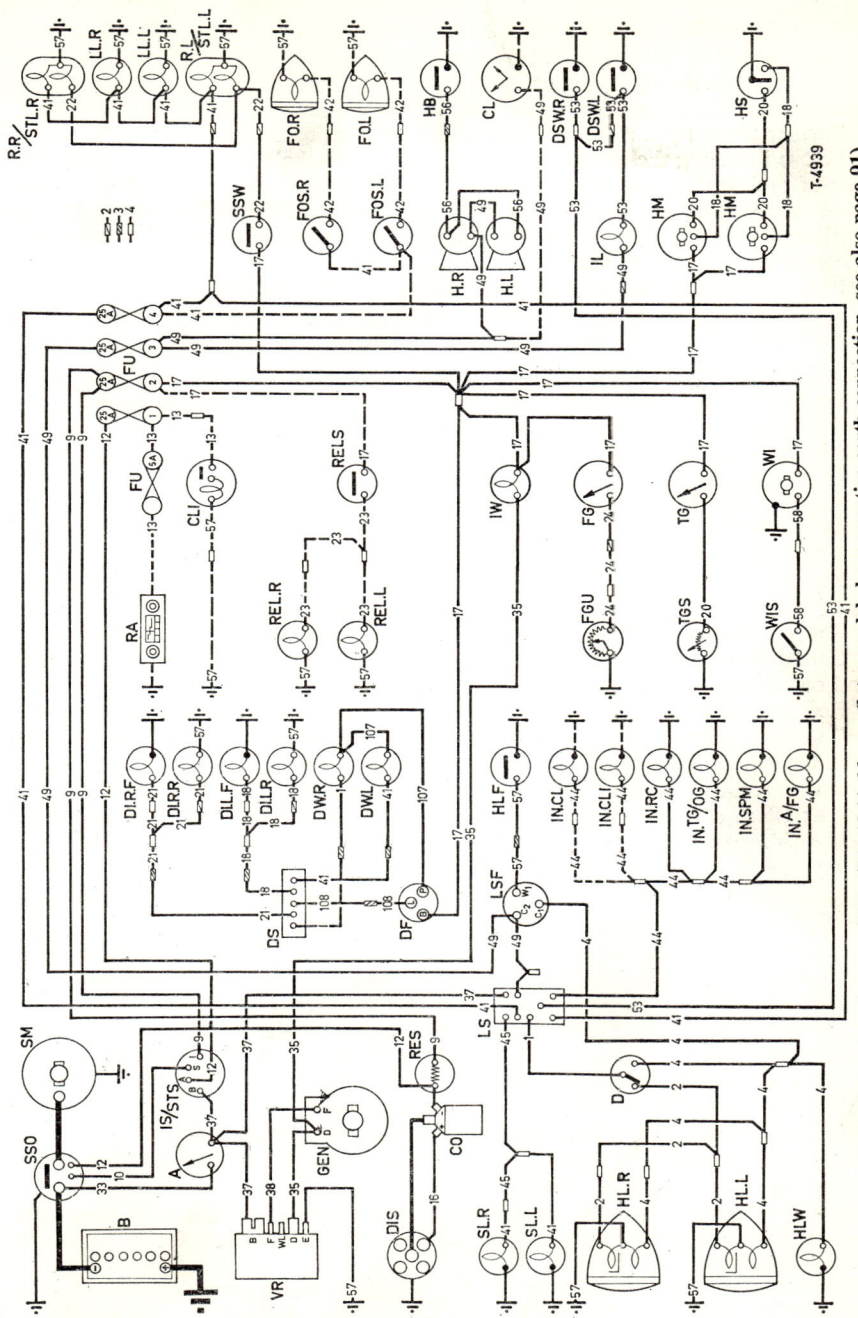

Fig. 51. Wiring diagram, VX 4/90, 1964-66   (later models have negative earth connection, see also page 91)

Place the new bush on end on one finger, thereby closing it at the bottom; now completely fill the bush with clean engine oil and place the thumb over the open end of the bush. Apply pressure until the oil is observed seeping through the porous wall of the bush. Repeat until the bush is entirely saturated; then install the bush.

Further assembly is a reversal of the dismantling procedure.

Before installing the commutator-end cover, place the brush springs against the side of each brush so that they can be retained in the retracted position. As the end-cover is properly seated against the yoke, replace the brush springs by unhooking them with a small hook or screwdriver and ensure that the brushes are properly pressed against the commutator.

Install the pulley-end bearing cover and the two through-bolts.

Install the pulley spacer, the Woodruff key, the pulley and the pulley nut.

For minimum permissible commutator diameter see *Technical Data*.

Starter motor: The starter motor is of the series-parallel-wound, four-pole, four-brush type, composed of a yoke, brush gear integral with the commutator-end cover and an armature with the drive mechanism, running in sintered bronze bushes.

Dismantling: After removal from the vehicle, the starter motor is dismantled as follows:

Remove the commutator cover band and the two through-bolts. Withdraw the drive-end cover, together with the armature, from the yoke.

Withdraw the two insulated brushes from their holders.

Remove the terminal nut, the plain washer and insulation washer from the terminal post. Remove the spacer from the insulating sleeve.

Remove the commutator-end cover and remove the terminal insulating sleeve.

Compress the heavy squared thrust spring on the drive and remove the circlip and collar; remove the thrust spring and thrust washer.

Remove the pinion and screwed sleeve assembly from the armature shaft.

It may be necessary to turn the pinion so that its internal splined washer lines-up with the splines on the shaft.

Testing and reconditioning:

NOTE: *When cleaning the parts of the starter motor, do not allow the armature of field coils to come in contact with any cleaning fluid, as otherwise the insulation will be impaired.*

Armature: Check whether the commutator is free of grooves, burnt spots or other irregularities; its surface should be smooth and regular. The commutator may be polished with very fine sandpaper. See *Technical Data* for minimum commutator diameter. Do not undercut the insulation between the commutator segments.

Check the armature windings with a suitable growler.

Brush gear: Check that the brushes can move freely in their holders; if necessary, clean each brush with a petrol-moistened rag or dress with a smooth file.

Check the brush spring tension with a spring balance.

If the brush length is less than the minimum permissible length of 0·30 in, replace with new brushes. Check the insulation of the positive brush holders.

Field coils: If one of the field coils shows a defect, the complete set must be replaced, as separate coils are not available.

Bearings: Carefully examine both bearing bushes for wear; replace as necessary. Before installation each bush should be saturated in oil, as detailed for the generator bush (see above).

Starter drive: Check the pinion sleeve nut and the screwed sleeve for wear or damage and check that the sleeve will spin freely through the nut.

Check the action of the thrust spring by comparing it with a new one.

Check whether the anti-drift spring in the pinion barrel is not broken or distorted.

Assembly: Assembly is a reversal of the dismantling operations. Install the commutator-end cover with the brush gear as outlined under *Generator* on page 78. Do not forget to install the thrust-washer(s) to the armature shaft. Before installation in the car it is advisable to check the operation of the starter motor on a test bench.

Windscreen-wiper motor:

Dismantling: Thoroughly clean the exterior of the motor, using solvent sparingly to prevent fouling the interior.

Remove the parking switch plate securing screw and swivel the plate clear.

Remove the nuts and washers from the through-bolts and withdraw the commutator-end cover with its insulator. Remove the shim and the insulating washer from the armature shaft.

Unsolder the brush wires, withdraw the wires from the brush holders and discard the brush springs.

Remove the inner nuts from the through-bolts and remove the brush support plate. Withdraw the brushes from their holders and discard the brushes.

Withdraw the armature and detach the thrust-ball located in a depression at the inner end of the shaft.

Checking and reconditioning: The interior of the motor should only be cleaned with air pressure. Never use liquid of any kind.

Armature: The commutator should be smooth and free of pits and burnt spots. If necessary, polish with very fine sandpaper and scrape any deposits from the commutator slots.

Carefully check the armature bearings and shaft for wear. The spherical bearing and the end-cover form one unit and should be replaced separately.

Drive out the old bearing bush and press-in the new bush so that it is flush with the housing face.

Test the armature for open circuits and possible earthed windings.

Field coils: The field coils must be tested for continuity and short circuits. Check that the insulation taping is in good order and that the coils are not loose on their pole shoes.

If necessary remove the field coils by unsoldering the connections at the switch plate and levering the assembly out of the housing with two screwdrivers.

When installing the field coils, make sure that the green and black wires can pass through the hole in the housing.

Assembly: Assembly is a reversal of the dismantling procedure; then test the motor by connecting the positive lead of a 12-volt test supply to the 'BATT' terminal and the negative lead to the 'SW' terminal on the body. Check the current drawn after 30 minutes of light running; this should be 2·5 amps.

Direction indicator switch:

Removal: Disconnect the battery, and with the aid of a screwdriver, prise off the horn ring cover.

Remove the steering wheel and the steering column lower cover securing screws. Disconnect the switch wiring connector at the main harness. On cars with instrument panel insulators it is necessary to withdraw the combined oil gauge and water temperature gauge unit in order to gain access to the connector. This also applies where, on earlier cars, the connector is not readily accessible.

Disconnect the ignition/starter wiring, loosen the set-screw securing the direction-indicator switch to the steering column.

Raise the steering column upper cover clear of the switch and remove the switch together with the steering cover lower cover.

Installation: Installation is a reversal of the above procedure. When installing the switch, ensure that the distance between the lug on the switch plate and the bottom of the chamfer on the steering shaft amounts to 0·70in.

Tighten the steering wheel nut to a torque of 38lb ft.

Lamp bulb replacement:

Headlamp sealed-beam units: Remove the headlamp surround and the three screws securing the sealed-beam unit retaining ring. Do not turn the lamp adjusting screws. Take the unit from its housing and disconnect the connector plug.

Installation is a direct reversal of the above procedure.

Headlamp adjustment, sealed-beam type: The headlamps should be set in accordance with the government regulations. Vertical adjustment is obtained by turning the topmost screw in the retaining ring in the desired direction; horizontal adjustment is obtained by turning both the screws located on the horizontal centre-line of the unit.

Bulb-type headlamp units, bulb replacement: Remove the headlamp surround. Firmly press-in the light unit and turn it counter-clockwise to release. Press-in and turn the bulb holder and withdraw, after which the bulb can be withdrawn.

On some lamp units, release the bulb socket retaining clips, withdraw the socket in order to replace the bulb.

Headlamp adjustment, bulb-type units: Vertical adjustment is obtained by turning the right-hand adjustment screw; the left-hand screw serves for horizontal adjustment.

Instrument lights, bulb replacement:
Withdraw the combined instrument cluster sufficiently to obtain access to the direction-indicator tell-tale and warning lamp bulb holders. When replacing the instrument lamp bulbs, complete removal of the gauge cluster will be necessary. Rotate the bulb socket counter-clockwise to align the locating tabs with the slots in the panel, and withdraw.

Instrument lamp bulbs on VX 4/90 models: Remove the facia moulding. Remove the combined ammeter/fuel gauge to gain access to the bulbs of this unit and the speedometer. The tachometer lamp bulbs are accessible after removal of the speedometer. The combined oil pressure and water temperature gauge lamp bulbs can be reached after removal of the tachometer.

Side-lamp and front direction-indicator lamp bulbs: Both lamp bulbs can be reached after their respective glasses have been removed. When replacing a side-lamp bulb it is necessary to remove the direction-indicator lamp lens first.

Tail, stop and direction-indicator lamp bulbs, all models: Access to either of these bulbs can be gained from inside the body; on estate cars the rear quarter trim panel must be removed. The reversing lamp bulb holder is located by two securing screws, accessible from the rear of the unit. These bulbs do not have to be turned for removal as they are of the capless type, which can be pulled straight out.

Rear number-plate lamp bulbs: Remove the reflector and the lens after removal of the two Phillips-headed screws. Remove the bulb and reinstall in reverse order.

Interior lamp bulb: The bulb is accessible after removal of the plastic lens. Remove the lens by squeezing its two longer sides together and pulling it downwards.

Technical Data
ENGINE

Engine model designations:
FC30: Victor 101, all models (engine prefix: 30FC/) $\left\{\begin{array}{l}\text{4-cyl., ohv}\\ \text{97·4 cu in (1594 cc)}\end{array}\right.$
FC31: VX4/90 (engine number prefix: 31FC/)
Cylinder head:
Material, FC30 engines: chromium cast-iron
        FC31 engines: aluminium
Cylinder-head attaching nuts, tightening sequence:

10	4	2	6	8	
7	5	1	3	9	Front

Compression ratio: FC30 engines: 9·0:1
          export option: 7·0:1
          FC31 engines: 9·3:1
Compression pressure, engine warm at cranking speed,
   throttle fully open, normal: 150–160 lb/sq in
            minimum: 125 lb/sq in
Maximum permissible difference between cylinders: 10 per cent
Minimum permissible cylinder-head height after
refacing the mating face, FC30 engines: 3·282 in
                 FC31 engines: 3·765 in
Nominal cylinder-head height, FC30 engines: 3·292–3·302 in
                 FC31 engines: 3·775–3·785 in
Maximum permissible mating face distortion:
             longitudinally: 0·005 in
             transversely: 0·003 in
Maximum permissible manifold mating face distortion: 0·002 in
Cylinder-head nut tightening torque (clean dry threads): 73 lb ft
Valves:
Valve head diameter, inlet: 1·432–1·442 in
             exhaust: 0·3102–0·3110 in
Valve stem diameter, inlet and exhaust: 0·3102–0·3110 in
Valve stem diameter on FC31 engines, exhaust: 0·3096–0·3103 in
Valve length, inlet: 4·707 in
           exhaust: 4·727 in
Valve length, FC31 engines, inlet: 5·179 in
              exhaust: 5·160 in
Maximum permissible clearance in guide,
          inlet and exhaust: 0·005 in
          FC31 engines: 0·004 in
Valve inclination on FC31 engines: 7°
Maximum permissible height of valve head above seat,
          inlet: 0·025 in
          exhaust: 0·035 in
Valve face angle: 44°
Valve lift: 0·335 in
Valve clearance, engine warm: 0·013 in
Valve seats:
Valve seat angle: 45°
Valve seat width, inlet: 0·035–0·060 in
           exhaust: 0·060–0·090 in
Valve guides:
Valve guide bore diameter, inlet and exhaust: 0·312–0·313 in

Valve guide projection above cylinder head, FC30 engines,

inlet and exhaust:	0·58 in
FC31 engines, inlet:	0·50 in
exhaust:	0·34 in

Valve springs:

Maximum fitted height, FC30 engines:	1·54 in
FC31 engines:	1·63 in
Free length, FC30 engines:	1·68 in
FC31 engines:	1·86 in
Spring load at length of 1·52 in,	35–55 lb
FC31 engines:	54–60 lb

Valve tappets:

Outer diameter:	0·8740–0·8735 in
Lift:	0·2332 in

Valve push-rods:

Push-rod length, inlet:	10·1 in
exhaust:	10·5 in

Valve rockers and rocker shaft:

Rocker-shaft diameter:	0·6672–0·6680 in
Maximum permissible valve rocker to rocker-shaft radial clearance:	0·004 in
Maximum permissible run-out of rocker shaft:	0·010 in

Timing gear:

Number of teeth, crankshaft sprocket:	21
camshaft sprocket:	42
Timing chain, type:	Duplex roller chain
Bore diameter crankshaft sprocket:	1·2572–1·2577 in
Bore diameter camshaft sprocket:	1·1255–1·1265 in
Crankshaft sprocket to crankshaft radial clearance:	0·0005–0·0020 in
Camshaft sprocket to camshaft radial clearance:	0·0005–0·0020 in

Valve timing diagram:

The valve timing diagram should be checked with the valves adjusted to their normal opening clearance of: 0·013 in

Inlet opens:	29° 36′ BTDC
Inlet closes:	76° 6′ ABDC
Exhaust opens:	71° 36′ BBDC
Exhaust closes:	34° 6′ ATDC

Camshaft:

Front bearing journal diameter:	1·9132–1·9137 in
Centre bearing journal diameter:	1·7570–1·7575 in
Rear bearing journal diameter:	1·7258–1·7263 in
Front bearing diameter:	1·9162–1·9172 in
Centre bearing diameter:	1·7600–1·7610 in
Rear bearing diameter:	1·7288–1·7298 in
Maximum permissible radial bearing clearance, front bearing:	0·0063 in
centre bearing:	0·0065 in
rear bearing:	0·0067 in
Camshaft end-float:	0·002–0·004 in
Camshaft thrust flange, thickness:	0·195–0·200 in

Crankshaft: The following specifications apply to crankshafts of FC30 engines only; in view of the special rolling procedure involved, crankshafts of FC31 engines are to be serviced and re-machined at the works only. For FC31 crankshaft, see page 87.

Crankshaft dimensions, FC30 engines:

Main bearing journal width, front:	1·800–1·828 in
centre:	1·123–1·127 in
rear:	1·480–1·490 in

Crankpin width:	1·065–1·069 in
Crankshaft radial clearance:	0·002–0·012 in
Maximum permissible run-out:	0·0015 in
Oil-seal journal diameter:	2·207–2·211 in
Main bearing clearance, front:	0·0005–0·0024 in
centre:	0·0005–0·0019 in
rear:	0·0007–0·0021 in
Crankshaft thrust-washer, thickness (standard):	0·091–0·093 in

Crankshaft dimensions, FC31 engine:

Main bearing journal diameter, front (standard):	2·1198–2·1208 in
centre (standard):	2·1200–2·1205 in
rear (standard):	2·1201–2·1206 in
Main bearing journal width, front:	1·800–1·820 in
centre:	1·123–1·127 in
rear:	1·480–1·490 in
Crankshaft end-float:	0·002·0·012 in
Maximum permissible run-out:	0·0015 in
Oil-seal journal diameter:	2·207–2·211 in
Thrust-washer thickness (standard):	0·091–0·093 in
Main bearing radial clearance, front:	0·0005–0·0024 in
centre:	0·0008–0·0022 in
rear:	0·0007–0·0021 in

Tightening torques, all engines:

Main bearing cap attaching bolts:	58 ft lb
Flywheel attaching bolts:	48 ft lb

Connecting rods:

Big-end bore diameter:	1·9945–1·9950 in
Piston-pin bush ground bore diameter, standard:	0·8664–0·8667 in
Piston-pin bush ground bore diameter, 0·003 in oversize:	0·8694–0·8697 in
Maximum permissible bend:	nil
Big-end bearing radial clearance:	0·0005–0·0025 in
Big-end bearing cap attaching nuts:	22 ft lb

Pistons:

Clearance in cylinder, measured at 0·90 in from bottom of cylinder at 90° angle with piston-pin bore axis:	0·0007–0·0012 in
Piston ring groove width, top ring:	0·0953–0·0963 in
centre ring:	0·0948–0·958 in
bottom ring:	0·1892–0·1902 in
Oversize pistons:	0·005, 0·020, 0·040 in*

*This oversize is not suitable for use with cylinder liners.
Gradation of standard size pistons: 0·00025 in to total value of 0·002 in (see table)
Identification of piston grade: stamped-in letter on piston top
Classification of oversize pistons: Y and W

Classification of oversize pistons:			Size	Grade	Piston diameter*
Size	*Grade*	*Piston diameter*	0·005in oversize	Y	3·21880–3·21930 in
	R	3·21280–3·21305 in		W	3·21930–3·21980 in
	TR	3·21305–3·21330 in	0·020in oversize:	Y	3·23380–3·23430 in
	B	3·21330–3·21355 in	(maximum for use with		
	TB	3·21355–3·21380 in	cylinder liners):	W	3·23430–3·23480 in
Standard size:	Y	3·21380–3·21405 in	0·040in oversize:	Y	3·25380–3·25430 in
	TY	3·21405–3·21430 in		W	3·25430–3·25480 in
	W	3·21430–3·21455 in	*Measured at 0·90 in from bottom of cylinder		
	TW	3·21455–3·21480 in	at 90° angle with piston pin bore axis.		

Piston rings:

Clearance in groove, top ring:	0·0015–0·0035 in
centre ring:	0·0010·0·0030 in
bottom ring:	0·0017–0·0037 in

Ring gap (all rings):   0·008–0·022 in
Cylinder block:
Cylinder block height, front cylinder-head mating face
   to main bearing cap mating face: 8·660–8·670 in
Minimum permissible cylinder block height: 8·650 in
Maximum permissible distortion of top face, longitudinally: 0·005 in
                            transversely: 0·003 in
Bore diameter for installing new dry liners: 3·353–3·354 in
Max. permissible piston oversize for use with dry liners: 0·020 in

Engine lubrication system:
Oil pressure of warm engine at 3000 rpm: 35–45 lb/sq in
Oil filter element type, FC30 engine: AC90 ⎱ see also
                  FC31 engine: AC73 ⎰ page 18
Oil pump type: gear type
Pump drive shaft diameter: 0·4982–4987 in
     end-float: 0·003–0·006 in
     radial clearance in housing: 0·0012–0·0025 in
Pump drive shaft diameter: 0·5007–0·5012 in
Fit in pump housing: zero to 0·0013 in
                           interference
Pump gear backlash: 0·006–0·012 in
Pump gear end-float in housing: 0·002–0·005 in
Pump gear radial clearance in housing: 0·0015–0·0035 in
Oil pressure relief valve spring, free length: 2·22 in
            spring tension at 1·72 in: 16 lb
Relief valve plunger to housing radial clearance: 0·0007–0·0025 in
Plunger diameter: 0·5605–0·5613 in

Ignition:
Firing order: 1–3–4–2
Static ignition timing: 9° BTDC
Location of timing mark: steel ball in flywheel in line with clutch housing aperture
Contact points gap (new points):   0·021–0·023 in
           (used points):   0·019 to 0·021 in
Breaker spring tension: 17–21 oz
Dwell angle: 35°–37°
Condenser capacity: 0·18–0·23 microfarad
Ignition distributor spindle, diameter: 0·4895–0·4900 in
           radial clearance: 0·0003–0·0013 in
           end-float: 0·002–0·005 in
           max. permissible end-float: 0·010 in
           shim thickness, upper: 0·029–0·033 in
                    lower: 0·056–0·066 in

Coil:
Make and type: Delco-Remy, oil-filled
Current consumption (distributor rpm):   0·78A at 1000
Primary coil resistance (at 20°C=68°F):   1·3 to 1·5 ohms
Coil resistor: 2 ohms at 20°C (68°F)

Spark plugs:

	FC30 *engine*	FC31 *engine*
Make and type:	AC, 14 mm	AC, 14 mm
Standard grade:	AC 43	AC 44XL
To prevent plug over-heating:	—	AC 43XL
To cure plug fouling:	AC 44–5V	AC 46XL

Electrode gap (all models):   0·028 to 0·032 in
Resistance of H.T. leads (resistance suppressor type)
  per foot length: 4000–8000 ohms

Fuel system:

Fuel tank capacity (approx.):		10 Imp gal (12 US gal)	
Fuel pump, make and type:		AC, FG	
Fuel pump pressure:		$2\frac{1}{2}$–$3\frac{1}{2}$ lb/sq in	
Pump diaphragm spring tension at 0·64 in:		$7\frac{1}{2}$–8 lb	
Carburettors:	*FC30*	*FC30*	*FC31*
Make and type:	Zenith 34 IV*	Zenith 34 IV**	Zenith 34 IV
Identification on float chamber:	C3066	C1843	
front carburettor:			1845F
rear carburettor:			1845R
Choke tube diameter:	28 mm (outer)	24 mm	24 mm (outer)
Main jet:	87	97	75
Compensating jet:	135	85	107
Pump jet:	55	55	55
Idling jet:	50	50	55
Air bleed jet:			
Air bleed screw:	- 3·0 mm	2·2 mm	2·4 mm
Float valve needle and seat:	1·75 mm	1·75 mm	1·5 mm
Float valve seat packing washer thickness:	2·0 mm	2·0 mm	2·0 mm
Float level***	6·5–7·5 mm	6·5–7·5 mm	6·5–7·5 mm

   * from engine No. 30FC/100111 with twin choke tubes.

  ** prior to engine No. 30FC/100111 with single choke.

*** with carburettor cover inverted measured between mating face and highest point of float upper edge.

Cooling system:

Cooling system operating pressure:	7 lb/sq in
Cooling system capacities:	see page 18
Thermostate type, early models:	bellows type
later models:	capsule type
Opening temperature, bellows type:	69–74°C (156–165°F)
capsule type:	80–84°C (177°–183°F)
Opening temperature, Western Thomson, capsule type:	85°–89°C (185°–192°F)

TRANSMISSION

Clutch:

Make and model:	Borg & Beck 8A6
Type and diameter:	single dry plate, 8 in
Number of clutch springs:	6
Number of damper springs in plate:	6
Friction lining thickness:	0·130 in
Friction area:	48·692 in
Throw-out bearing, type: single ball-bearing, permanently pre-packed with grease	

Three-speed gearbox:

Main drive shaft diameter:	1·1808–1·1813 in
Bore diameter of main drive shaft bearing cover:	2·4412–2·4418 in
Mainshaft diameter:	1·0002–1·0007 in
Main drive shaft spigot bearing bore diameter:	1·1807–1·1811 in
Number of spigot bearing needle rollers:	24
Bore diameter, first- and second-speed pinions:	1·4760–1·4770 in
Gear cluster assembly, total length:	6·1410–6·1440 in
Gear cluster adjustment shims, thickness:	0·0615–0·0635 in
Gear cluster end-float:	0·0048·0·0177 in
Secondary shaft diameter, front end:	0·7045–0·7052 in
rear end:	0·6701–0·6708 in
Number of gear cluster needle rollers, front:	26
rear:	25

Reverse speed pinion end-float:	0·0040–0·0139 in
Inside diameter reverse-speed pinion bush:	0·7820–0·7830 in
Fit of reverse-speed pinion shaft in housing, front:	0–0·0013 in
rear:	0·0002–0·0015 in
Shifter-fork in synchronizer sleeve, groove clearance:	0·0080–0·0160 in

Four-speed gearbox (where different from three-speed gearbox):

First-speed pinion bore diameter:	1·3510–1·3525 in
First-speed pinion bush outer diameter:	1·3484–1·3490 in
Mainshaft journal for first-speed pinion bush diameter:	1·0625–0·0630 in
Gear cluster assembly, total length:	
Gear cluster assembly, total length:	7·141–7·144 in

Rear axle differential:

Axle shaft diameter for rear wheel bearing, all models:	1·1817–1·1822 in
Interference fit of wheel bearing on axle shaft:	0·0006–0·0016 in
Wheel bearing bore diameter in rear axle tube,	
FCW and FCG models:	2·8346–2·8358 in
all other models:	2·4404–2·4410 in
Interference fit of rear wheel bearings in axle tube,	
FCW and FCG models:	0 to +0·0017 in
all other models:	+0·0006 to —0·0005 in
Fit of pinion front bearing on pinion shaft:	+0·002 to —0·0007 in
Interference fit of pinion front bearing in housing:	0·0003–0·0019 in
Fit of pinion rear bearing on pinion shaft:	0·0003–0·0012 in
Interference fit of pinion rear bearing in housing:	0·0003–0·0012 in
Available shims for differential bearing adjustment:	0·100, 0·101, 0·003 in
Differential bearing pre-load, measured on differential	
housing periphery with spring balance, near bearings:	2·5–3 lb
used bearings:	1 lb
Differential pinion shaft diameter:	0·6243–0·6248 in
Differential pinion end-float on shaft:	0·0027–0·0053 in
Interference fit pinion shaft in differential housing:	+0·0013 to —0·0003 in
Radial clearance of differential side gears in housing bore:	0·002–0·005 in
Maximum permissible differential housing run-out,	
measured at crownwheel mating face:	0·001 in
Maximum permissible run-out of crownwheel, fitted and	
measured on the back side:	0·002 in
Pinion to crownwheel backlash:	
Bolt tightening in ft lb (clean, dry threads),	
differential bearing cap bolts:	24
crownwheel attaching bolts:	38
Pinion bearing pre-load, measured at final drive flange,	
new bearings:	4 in lb
used bearings:	8–11 in lb
Pinion depth adjustment shims:	0·003, 0·005, 0·010 in
Interference fit of differential bearings on	
differential housing:	0·0014–0·0025 in
Interference fit of differential bearings in housing:	+0·0007 to —0·0005 in

CHASSIS

Front suspension:

Interference fit, inner wheel bearing in hub:	0·0010–0·0025 in
Interference fit, outer wheel bearing in hub:	0·0010–0·0026 in
Fit of inner wheel bearing on stub axle:	+0·003– +0·0012 in
Fit of outer wheel bearing on stub axle:	+0·0002– +0·0015 in
Maximum permissible number of shims for camber and	
castor angle adjustment, on top fulcrum shaft:	6
on lower fulcrum shaft:	2

Brake backing plate attaching nut tightening torque: 24 lb ft
Riding height, front: see page 61

Rear suspension:
Number of spring leaves, saloon: 3
estate car: 4
Riding height, rear (also refer to page 61): 9·25 to 10·25

Steering gear:
Make: Burman or Cam Gears Ltd.
Type: recirculating ball
Steering gear ratio $\left.\right\}$ straight-ahead position 15·7 : 1
Total ratio 18·0 : 1
Number of steering wheel turns, lock to lock: 4
Oil capacity and lubricant: see page 20
Number of worm bearing balls (each bearing): 10
Number of main nut assembly balls: 12
Worm bearing pre-load, pitman arm removed, measured
at steering wheel rim: 2–8 oz
Steering gear total pre-load, measured at steering wheel rim: 12–16 oz
Tightening torques (clean, dry threads):
Steering box mounting bolts: 25 ft lb
Pitman shaft nut: 63 ft lb
Steering wheel nut: 38 ft lb
Steering idler arm mounting: 25 ft lb

Disc brakes, front (Girling):
Brake disc diameter: 9·06 in
Brake disc thickness: 0·375 to 0·380 in
Maximum permissible run-out: 0·004 in
Brake pad lining and area (each pad): DON 2212: 25 cm
Minimum permissible brake pad thickness: 0·12 in

Vacuum servo unit
Diaphragm diameter: 5·5 in
Power ratio: 2·2 : 1

Brake master cylinder:
Brake master cylinder inside diameter: 0·75 in

Drum brakes:
Brake drum inside diameter: 9·000–9·005 in
Maximum permissible inside diameter: 9·060 in
Maximum permissible run-out (radial): 0·002 in

Wheels and tyres:
Maximum permissible lateral and radial run-out measured on rim: 0·040 in
Tyre sizes and pressures: see page 20

ELECTRICAL
Electrical system voltage: 12 volts
Battery earthing, 1964–66 positive, 1966–67 negative
Battery: Standard type: 38 Amp at 20-hour rate
Special order: 54 Amp at 20-hour rate

Generator:	*standard*	*heavy duty*
Make and model:	Lucas, C40 or C40/1	Lucas; C40L
Cut-in speed and voltage:	1450 rpm (max.) at 13 V	1350 rpm (max.) at 13 Volts
Output:	22 Amp and 13·5 Volts at 2250 rpm	25 Amp and 13·5 Volts at 2275 rpm
Field coil resistance:	6 ohms	5·9 ohms

Minimum permissible commutator diameter (after skimming),
up to October 1964: 1·45 in
from November 1964: 1·43 in

G

Voltage regulator:

Type: 3-coil Lucas RB340

Air gap (armature to core):   0·052–0·056 in

Voltage regulator, open-circuit setting: 14·4–15·0 V at 10°C (50°F), 14·2–14·8 V
    at 20°C (68°F), 14·0–14·6 V at 30°C (86°F), 13·8–14·4 V at 40°C (104°F).

Current regulator:

Air gap (armature to core):   0·052–0·056 in

Load setting, generator C40 and C40/1:   21–23 Amp

               generator C40L: 24–26 Amp

Field resistance: 55–65 ohms

Cut-out relay:

Cut-in voltage: 12·6–13·4 volts

Reverse current: 8 Amp (maximum)

Air gap (armature to core):   0·035–0·045 in

Moving contact follow-through: point just touching with 0·015 in air gap

Starter motor:

Make and model: Lucas M35G/1

Minimum permissible commutator diameter: 1·281 in (after skimming)

Brush spring tension, new brushes (max.):   34–36 oz

           used brushes (min.):   25 oz

Minimum permissible brush length: 0·30 in

Current drawn at 9500–11,000 rpm: 45 Amp

Stall torque and stall-torque current: 7·7 lb ft at 330–350 Amp
                                    7·1 to 7·5 volts

Starter solenoid switch:

Make and type: Lucas 2ST

Lamp bulb data:

Headlamps: *Watts*

  Right-hand drive, except Continental: 60/45

  Right- and left-hand drive, Continental: 45/40

  Left-hand drive, except Continental unified
    European and USA: 50/40

  Left-hand drive, unified European: 45/40

  Left-hand drive, USA: 60/45

Sidelamps, number-plate lamps & reversing lamps: 6

Rear/stoplamps: 6/21

Direction-indicator lamps, front and rear: 21

Direction-indicator, interior: 2·2

Warning light bulbs and instrument lights: 2·2

Interior light (dome light):   11

Windscreen-wiper motor:

Make and type: Delco 258, 12-volt

Stall torque: 4·75 ft lb at 12 volts

Current consumption (when warm):   2·5 Amp

Fuses:

Location of fuse-holder: on fire wall in engine compartment

Fuse-protected accessories (four fuses):

No. 1: radio and cigar lighter*

No. 2: heater blower motor, stoplamps, direction-indicator lamps, warning lights,
    fuel gauge, water temperature gauge, reversing lamps and windscreen-wiper motor*

No. 3 interior light, headlamp flasher and horns

No. 4: tail lamps, number-plate lamp, instrument lights and cigar lighter illumination

*On later models the windscreen-wiper motor is connected to fuse No. 1. The wire
    running from the 'BATT' terminal of the windscreen-wiper motor to the three-
    way junction is deleted, and a new wire (colour white/green) runs directly from
    the 'BATT' terminal to fuse No. 1.

GENERAL FAULT FINDING CHART
FOR PETROL ENGINES

Some items in this chart are not applicable to every make of petrol engine

Engine will not start

A. Starter does not crank engine

Battery run down	*Recharge; replace if defective*
Battery posts and terminals loose or corroded	*Clean and tighten. If badly corroded, soak with water to facilitate removal and avoid damage to the battery posts*
Faulty starter switch or solenoid, if fitted; broken battery cable or loose connection	*Check wires and cables; check solenoid and switch, replace if defective*
Starter motor defective	*Repair or replace*
Starter drive stuck (starter will run, but does not crank engine)	*Clean and if necessary repair or replace*
Starter drive pinion jammed with starter ring gear	*Free by rotating squared end of starter spindle with a spanner*

B. Starter cranks engine slowly

Battery partly run down	*Recharge; replace if defective*
Loose or corroded connections	*Clean and tighten*
Faulty starter switch or solenoid; partly broken cable or loose connection	*Check wires and cables; check solenoid and switch, replace if necessary*
Starter motor defective	*Repair or replace*

C. Starter cranks engine, but engine will not start

Trouble in ignition system:

No spark at plugs:

Moisture on spark plugs, ignition distributor, coil and wires (this trouble often occurs after parking overnight in foggy or rainy weather)	*Clean and dry. Avoid recurrence by coating wires, distributor rotor, cap, coil and spark plug insulators with moisture-proof lacquer*
Spark plugs flooded, due to excessive use of choke	*Start engine on full throttle. If this does not help, clean plugs. With plugs removed, turn over the crankshaft a few times to blow the accumulated fuel from the cylinders*

Spark plugs oiled-up	*Clean; if necessary replace*
Spark plug insulator cracked	*Replace*
Spark plug gap too wide or too close	*Reset gap*
No spark at distributor:	
Loose, broken or shorted low-tension lead between coil and/or inside distributor	*Check and tighten; also check internal leads in distributor. These leads sometimes break inside their insulation, and the break is not always visible. Pull carefully on one end; a broken lead will stretch*
Cracked rotor or distributor cap	*Replace*
Contact breaker points dirty, worn or maladjusted	*Clean and adjust; if necessary replace*
Carbon brush in distributor cap not making contact	*Free; if necessary replace*
Faulty condenser	*Replace*
No spark at coil:	
High-tension lead loose or broken	*Replace*
Broken or loose low-tension leads or faulty ignition switch	*Check wiring, repair or replace; check switch, replace if defective*

D. Starter cranks engine, but engine will not start

Trouble in fuel system:

No petrol in carburettor:

Empty fuel tank	*Fill up. If necessary, check and repair or replace fuel gauge*
Obstructed or damaged fuel pipe	*Clean; if necessary repair or replace*
Air leak in petrol line	*Check and repair or replace. Pay special attention to flexible fuel line (if fitted). If flexible fuel line is porous, a temporary 'get-you-home' repair can often be made by securely wrapping the line with friction tape or rubbing with hard soap*
Fuel filter clogged	*Clean and refit with new gasket. Always carry a spare gasket and a glass filter bowl, if so equipped*

Fuel pump defective	*Repair or replace. If electric pump does not function, lightly tap pump housing until ticking resumes*
Petrol in carburettor:	
Jets clogged	*Clean; blow out with air (never use wire to clean jets)*
Float needle stuck	*Clean or replace*
Carburettor flooded	*Clean float needle valve; if necessary replace. If this trouble persists, check fuel pump pressure*
Choke control faulty	*Repair or replace*
Air leak at inlet manifold or carburettor base	*Check nuts and bolts for tightness; if necessary replace gaskets*
Water or dirt in carburettor	*Clean. If this trouble persists, check rubber hose in fuel tank filler neck for damage or looseness, causing water to enter tank*

NOTE: *If ignition system and carburettor are in order, yet the engine will not start, check timing.*

Engine starts but does not run properly

E. Engine misfires	
Ignition trouble:	
Spark plug or coil leads loose or damaged	*Tighten; replace if necessary*
Incorrect spark plug gap	*Regap*
Cracked spark plug insulator	*Replace faulty spark plug*
Spark plug oiled-up	*Clean, if necessary replace with spark plug of correct type. If trouble persists, check for mechanical trouble*
Cracked distributor cap	*Replace*
Loose connection in primary circuit	*Check and repair. Also check, and if necessary replace, ignition switch. In rare cases the ammeter has been found to be the cause of this trouble, due to faulty internal connection*
Distributor otherwise faulty	*See* **C**
Trouble in fuel system:	*See* **D**

Mechanical trouble:

Incorrect valve clearance	*Adjust*
Valve sticking	*Try to free by pouring a gum solvent of good quality into carburettor air intake; if not successful, dismantle and repair*
Valve spring broken	*Replace. Usually the valve concerned will have to be ground*
Worn piston, piston rings and cylinder or burnt valve; cylinder-head gasket blown	*Test compression; if too low, dismantle for repairs*

F. Engine starts and stops

Trouble in ignition or fuel system:	*See* **C** *and* **D**
Obstructed exhaust system	*Check and repair or replace*

G. Engine runs on wide throttle only

Idle jet clogged or mixture improperly adjusted	*Clean idle jet and/or idle air bleed; adjust*
Valve sticking or burnt; valve spring broken; other mechanical trouble	*Check and repair. Pay special attention to heat riser, if so equipped, since a burnt heat riser will cause exhaust gas to enter intake manifold. This will sometimes cause backfiring in carburettor*

H. Lack of power

Ignition too far retarded or other ignition trouble	*Check and correct (see* **C***)*
Obstructed exhaust system	*Dented exhaust pipe and/or muffler Dislocated baffle plate in muffler Replace*
Trouble in fuel system	*Check and correct (see* **D***)*
Loss of compression	*Test compression; if found to be too low, check valve clearance. If valve clearance is properly adjusted and compression is still low, check for other mechanical trouble, such as burnt valves and/or worn pistons, rings and cylinders*
Dragging brakes	*Check and correct. Essentially this is not an engine trouble*